THE REAL ENTREPRENEUR

How to simplify, grow and **enjoy** your business

LISA ZEVI

RETHINK PRESS

First published in Great Britain in 2019 by Rethink Press
(www.rethinkpress.com)

Printed by CPI Group (UK) Ltd, Croydon CR0 4YY

Praise

'All Lisa's business enthusiasm and knowledge spills onto the pages of this book. She has a real curiosity to understand and problem-solve and an infectious desire that makes you want to work with her. She doesn't always spell out what I want to hear, nor does she follow the party line, but the feedback is always genuine, insightful and she usually gives me something to think about that wasn't on the table before. She may be the COO in a BOX but she is frequently outside the box! Bravo on a great read.'
— **Graham Brown**
   Managing Director of Forces Recruitment Solutions

'This is a book about getting things done and applying real world learnings and tools to common problems facing businesses in the growth stage.'
— **Julian Cork**
   COO of Landbay

'This book will help entrepreneurs get real and focus on what really matters, offering a balanced blend of theory, insightful tools, case studies and exercises.'
— **Francesca Polo**
   COO and Co-Founder of Vastari

'*The REAL Entrepreneur* is a wonderful distillation of Lisa's years of experience in making businesses better. Reading this book is like having Lisa by your side, helping you grow your business and improving it along the way.'
— **Andy Pieroux**
Founder and Managing Director of Walpole Partnership

'Having built a number of businesses, I understand the frustration of trying to operate outside of your flow. This book will help any business owner to build their business more effectively, whilst enjoying more of the journey.'
— **Nick Carlile**
Co-Founder of Shepherd Cox

'Having experienced Lisa's methods through one-to-one and group coaching, I was expecting great things from her book. Once again, she has delivered. *The REAL Entrepreneur* is a must read for all of us who are struggling with running a company and managing a team. Lisa's style is clear, concise and always engaging, and the insights I have received from her methods have already allowed me to communicate more effectively with my staff and avoid panic even in difficult situations. The lady is a star.'
— **Marcella Puppini**
International Recording Artist and Founder of The Puppini Sisters

'For me, this book brings the practical world of business together. When I got my MBA, I knew the questions to ask across most business areas, but it was not always clear how to engage with the problems I faced. This book quickly transitions from problems into tactics and techniques by opening up so many avenues with clear implementation strategies. I can honestly say that this book makes my MBA useful – it should be required reading for all students!'

    — Roger Press
        Founder and Managing Director of
        Classical World and Academic Rights Press

'As business owners and entrepreneurs, we work hard at running and growing our businesses. We risk feeling overwhelmed, getting stuck and not really doing what we love. It can be hard to take a step back and reflect on the development of our business and our role in it. *The REAL Entrepreneur* provides a valuable and practical framework to help us do exactly that. I enjoyed reading it and am currently using its methods on a weekly basis. I highly recommended *The REAL Entrepreneur* to any owner of a small business.'

    — Jan van Veen
        Founder and Managing Director of
        moreMomentum

'Lisa writes with a clear and engaging voice. Her REAL model creates order from chaos. Read it cover to cover or dip in and out, either way it will provide answers and direction. Lisa has created a book that you can use to take real action!'

— **Isobel Colson**
Founder of Get Going Coaching

'Lisa has written this fantastic, sensible, easy to read, friendly and no nonsense handbook for business owners like me! It gives us practical ideas on getting back in touch with why we began our businesses and, just as importantly, focusing on the what and how we can grow them using her REAL model. REAL enables us to focus on one area at a time to help us reduce overwhelm. This week I'm focused on Accountability!'

— **Ann Skidmore**
Managing Director, Ann Skidmore Associates

Contents

For anyone who has ever wanted to grow, move or change.
May you play to your strengths, speak your truth and
build a business that works for you.

Dear Lisa,

Wishing you success and
happiness in everything you do.

Lisa

Foreword

What if there was a real-world formula to growing a scalable and sustainable business that made it easy for you to take action and get real results?

I believe that this book offers you that opportunity. But for that opportunity to turn into confidence, customers and cash flow you are going to need to make a commitment to yourself to master this material. To really take the time to understand and implement the abundance of growth ideas packed into the pages you now hold in your hand.

Are you up for that? I ask because most people who purchase books like this seldom get past Chapter Three in my experience, which is why most entrepreneurs rarely succeed, they lack the ability and stamina to go the distance.

How can I say that with such certainty?

Well, over the last 15 years I've coached, consulted and trained with well over 5,000 business owners, leaders and salespeople from different industries and across different countries. They are united by one burning desire: to grow their business results without it consuming their life, their energy, their relationship, their health and all their wealth.

As a fellow entrepreneur, who has at times let his companies consume far too much of his life, cash and energy, the lessons in this book may well save you from a serious illness like the one I suffered and survived a few short years ago. It's an experience I would not want you or your family to have to go through and rebuild from.

When you picked up this book you made a decision, a decision to get real with yourself and your business. To stop believing your own marketing hype and start looking at the core fundamentals that need to be in place for your business to grow to the next level. Lisa is the perfect person to take you on that journey.

We first met a few years ago when a property investor client of mine introduced us. Lisa was looking for a profiling tool to help her clients understand themselves better so that they could build high-performing teams and successful businesses. What struck me during our conversation was how well she understood herself and the tool, before she shifted into lots and lots of 'how to' questions which enabled her to evaluate and then use it to create a profound and positive impact for her clients.

In the months and years that have followed, I've coached and collaborated with Lisa as part of both my F12 Mastermind and as a Certified Team Dynamics Trainer. I am always impressed with her unique perspective on entrepreneurs as one of the world's leading coaches and experts on how CEOs (Chief Executive Officers) and COOs (Chief Operating Officers) work together.

This view, from the number two seat if you will, is very rare and really helps an entrepreneur to understand the key leverage tools they will need to deploy to truly scale their company, and perhaps even reach an exit point of sale. These include REAL Systems, a REAL Team with REAL Accountability, a REAL Plan and REAL Leadership!

Lisa brilliantly brings these strategies alive with extracts from her interviews with highly successful business owners building exciting and industry-disrupting brands. The insights from these interviews are like little nuggets of golden value sprinkled throughout the book that keep you wanting to read on and undercover the next to add to your treasure chest.

Packed with 'how to' tips, tactics and tools you can deploy quickly and easily in your business, it really is like having Lisa alongside you as your COO to guide you through the challenges and changes you'll face running and growing your company.

One of the biggest myths in our culture is that all successful people are 'self-made'. We often hear the term 'self-made millionaire', yet the reality is that nobody does it on their own and the smartest and most successful people ask for the support they need.

To succeed as an entrepreneur, you are going to need to become more energised and resilient. If there's one thing I can promise you, it is that life will beat you up and knock you down on this journey. The question is, do you have the skills and the strength to get back up again and keep going and growing? This is where Lisa delivers with her chapters on 'how to' become more resilient and have more energy as the living leader of your brand. This is a subject that I feel has just not had enough attention paid to it over the years. If all you do is apply the key lessons and learnings from these chapters, your odds of achieving your goals without giving up will skyrocket.

During my experience of working closely with Lisa and having had an opportunity to read and digest the vast value packed into this book, I know what a treat you have in store as you read on. She really does know how to help you simplify, grow and enjoy your business.

This book can be a REAL turning point in your journey as an entrepreneur. I hope it is, and I wish you all the success you are prepared to learn and work for.

Paul Avins
CEO & Chief Innovation Officer – Team Dynamics Global
www.TeamDynamics.com & www.PaulAvins.com

Preface

'The only way to do great work is to love what you do.'
— Steve Jobs, co-founder of Apple Inc.

Once there was a woman who loved to sew. Let's call her Sally. She made dresses and shirts and toys and loved coming up with new creations for her friends and family. She loved working with different fabrics to make intricate and beautiful patterns, and she was always trying new things. Her favourite thing was customising clothes and making them into something unique. She was always willing to share her ideas and loved helping other people get creative.

One day, a friend came to Sally and asked if she would make a dress for her daughter's birthday. The friend offered to cover the cost of the materials, and Sally got to work. She created the most amazing party dress but didn't stop there. She made decorations for the party and toys for the children to play with. She put together kits for the children so that they could create pretty things of their own. Sally's friend was ecstatic. Her daughter loved the dress and didn't want to take it off. Some of the boys at the party made their own waistcoats by sticking pieces of material onto the cutouts that Sally had put into their kits. Sally felt happy but exhausted – it had been a lot of work. After the party, Sally got several enquiries about creating clothes and toys for other events. She agreed delightedly but decided to get someone to help her pull everything together.

Several months passed with Sally getting more and more enquiries from friends of friends, all of whom had heard about her exquisite and imaginative creations. She took on more people to help her out while she focused on creating new things. She found that she loved learning what customers wanted and coming up with interesting ways to excite and delight them. For each new customer she would create something different – a new material, colour or design. She made robot kits, reversible skirts and shirts, and unicorn costumes that even more grown-up children loved to try. Her customers raved about how her creations encouraged children to use their imagination as they adapted the clothes and toys to whatever they wanted. A web designer friend offered to create a website for her and also set Sally up with some social media accounts. Another friend, who was a lawyer, advised her to create a company and get proper contracts in place with her team. Sally didn't know anything about marketing, contracts or companies but was determined to learn. She enrolled on several courses and started reading everything she could get her hands on. Every day there was something new to read, to learn and to do.

Sally decided that working from her living room wasn't practical. She had boxes of materials everywhere and found it hard to switch off from work in the evenings. She decided to rent a place where she could work and take on a few of the people full-time. She hired an accountant and created her company. Her friend helped her put together contracts for her people and negotiate with the manufacturers of different fabrics and materials that Sally wanted to use. She tried to apply everything she'd learned but felt exposed and out of her comfort zone. There was so much to sort out – desks, computers, phones, storage bins for all her fabrics and materials, new equipment to order, an online store on her website to create. She felt under pressure all the time and was convinced that she should be doing a better job at managing everything.

Meanwhile, more and more people wanted her beautiful creations at their events and her team was growing. She found some great young people and taught them how to sew, create kits and decorate everything to make it look beautiful. As well as training her team, she was dealing with all the customers, running all the events and trying to do a bit of social media on the side. She took every opportunity to spread the word about her amazing products and found that she loved talking to people about sewing and creative play. Her online sales took off and soon she was shipping products all over the world. More and more people not only wanted to buy her creations but also wanted to learn how to make them themselves. A friend of hers offered to shoot some videos of her explaining how to make the kits and offering suggestions on how to customise clothing and toys. He talked to her about webinars and membership sites and subscriptions, and Sally found herself feeling increasingly out of her depth, trying to learn and absorb as much as she could. She loved the idea of growing her business online but couldn't see how she'd ever be able to manage everything.

Sally's days got longer and longer, and she found herself feeling overwhelmed and exhausted. She found herself lying awake at night, running through an ever-increasing 'to-do' list and worrying about all the things she might be missing. She took on more people but all the decisions kept coming back to her. She couldn't understand why her team didn't take on more of the responsibility. They had so many questions for her every day, and there were always so many decisions to make. She noticed that people were making mistakes, and sometimes the same task ended up being done by more than one person. She tried to deal with as much as she could but felt that time was always against her. Her business felt more and more chaotic and confused.

One day, her bank called to tell her that her account was overdrawn. She couldn't understand how that could be when she had so many customers. When she looked at her account, she was horrified to find that several of her customers hadn't paid her for parties she'd supplied several weeks before, and yet she'd had to pay out a large amount to a fabric supplier. She phoned her customers and got several of them to pay. Realising that she hadn't looked at her bank account for weeks, she resolved to do that more regularly. A few days later, one of her team resigned and told her that the work environment was too chaotic and confusing and that Sally never had time for any of them. Sally had hardly spoken to members of her team in weeks, and she resolved to fix that. The next week, she got a call telling her that her IT and telephony guy had been taken ill with stress. In a panic, Sally discovered that she didn't know any of her account passwords or who her suppliers were. When she looked into it further, she realised that she didn't even own the domain her website was hosted on. It felt like a different issue popped out of the woodwork each day – a new thing that she had to learn about, a new problem to solve.

She tried her best to keep up with all the customers who left messages wanting to talk to her, but she didn't always manage to get back to them quickly enough.

One day, she returned a call that had been left two days earlier and the person told her that they'd found someone else. Sally was upset and resolved to return calls more quickly, not knowing how she was going to manage that. She knew that her team were unhappy, but she didn't have time to think about how to fix it.

Sally started getting home later and later. Her husband told her he was worried about her and her children told her they missed her. Her friends tried to get her to meet up, but Sally kept turning them down so most stopped calling. Sally didn't know what to do. She felt like she was running just to keep still, without a moment to even think straight. She was sure that at any moment she would get completely overwhelmed with everything and it would drown her. She told her husband that things would get better, but when he asked her what was going to change, she couldn't answer. She told herself that she just needed to work harder and learn more and then everything would be OK. Her website designer friend suggested that she get some help or advice about how to manage and grow her business, but Sally was convinced that she could figure it out herself.

Then she got a call from a customer telling her that she was disappointed with the quality of the kits and outfits Sally's team had provided at her son's birthday party. She told her that the reason she'd come to Sally in the first place was because of the personal touch her friends had told her about. She'd wanted something unique and different but felt that what she'd received was generic. She also wasn't happy with some of Sally's team, who she felt had been disorganised and stressed.

Sally was devastated. She berated herself for being so rubbish at everything. She wasn't managing the finances, she wasn't managing the team and she wasn't keeping her customers happy. She told herself that she should never have started out in business, that she had let herself and everyone else down. She felt guilty that she hadn't seen enough of her husband and children or her friends. She couldn't remember the last time she'd actually created anything or sat down with a customer and spent time understanding what they really wanted. She felt like a complete failure.

She told her team that she was going out for a walk, and she took herself to her favourite spot by the river. A million things ran through her mind. She felt sure that there was an answer, a way through, but she just couldn't see it. She sat on a bench, lost in her thoughts, eyes closed, feeling the sun on her face. Then she realised that someone was sitting quietly beside her and she opened her eyes. The woman asked her if she was OK, and Sally started to pour out her troubles. It felt so good to talk, to let it all out. The woman asked a few questions but mainly stayed silent, listening to everything that Sally was telling her. Sally felt guilty and slightly embarrassed for sharing all her problems with a complete stranger, but the woman smiled and encouraged her to keep going. When Sally got to the end of the story, the woman asked her, 'What do you love doing?' The question frustrated Sally – she just wanted all the stress and hassle to go away. The woman gently repeated her question, and this time Sally told her that she loved creating new and pretty things to make other people happy and that she loved helping others be creative. That was why she'd started her business but now she had no time at all to do what she loved.

The woman asked her what she wanted from her life, why she was in business and what she was hoping to achieve. Sally's face lit up as she talked about training her team and showing people how to sew. She described being able to delight and surprise her customers and how much she loved the process of coming up with new materials, colours and designs. She said that she would love to run online courses, write books about sewing and creative play and do live demonstrations of how to customise garments and let your imagination run wild. The woman asked her about her customers, and Sally smiled and then frowned. She told the woman that she had more customers than she knew how to deal with and she was devastated to be letting them down.

The woman asked about her team and what each of them did and could do, and as Sally talked through each person and thought about their strengths and capabilities, she began to realise that the solution might be right in front of her. She was trying to do too many things and not focusing on the bits that she loved and was good at. She had a great team, but she wasn't using them to share the load, and she wasn't focusing on building her business but instead just running from one thing to another. She was so stressed that she wasn't thinking clearly. She realised that she needed to start with herself – she wasn't looking after herself at all, and if she couldn't think clearly, then there was no chance of saving her business, let alone growing it. She told the woman that she had no idea how to get out of the mess she was in. The woman suggested that she make a long list of everything on her plate and start thinking about *who* rather than *how*. She stood up, said goodbye and was gone before Sally could thank her.

Sally felt deflated and confused but couldn't face going back to the office. She decided to try what the woman had suggested. For a long time, she sat on the bench by the river making a list. She thought about all the things that were taking up her time and wrote down each one. She listed all the things that people were asking her to decide and all the people she wanted and needed to talk to. She took out her phone and wrote down all the types of calls she'd made and received in the last few weeks. She looked at her email and listed all the different types of email that she received and sent on a regular basis. Then she thought about all the things she really wanted to do and the things that people were chasing her to do that she just hadn't found the time for and added them to the list. She also wrote down all the things that she was stuck with or avoiding.

When she was done, Sally stared at the list, feeling a weird combination of overwhelm and calm. At least everything was out of her head and she could see it. Working through each item on the list, she tried to think about *who* could either do it or help with it, and *who* might have some information or contacts that would help move things forward.

Suddenly she realised that it would be better to do this with her team. She headed back to the shop, got everyone together and told them that she wanted to start doing things differently. She shared the list with the team, who started to offer suggestions and volunteer to do things. Sally quickly found herself feeling overwhelmed again. One of her supervisors, Oliver, asked Sally if it would be helpful if he started writing everything down and capturing who was going to do what. The team crowded around the whiteboard and started talking animatedly. The conversation flowed and the energy was amazing. Every now and then Oliver would turn to her and ask her a question – 'Did she want to be involved in this? Would she prefer to handle that?'

Sally watched in astonishment as her team took up the challenge – each person choosing the items that played to their strengths. She wondered if she should feel bad that most of the things on the board had someone else's name against them. The only things that had her name against them were things that she loved – teaching people, talking about creative play, coming up with new creations and setting the vision for her business. She would never have imagined that asking *who* rather than *how* could have such an impact, but here it was happening right in front of her eyes. She felt a wave of optimism sweep over her. She felt that anything was possible as long as she wasn't on her own. She wished that she'd asked the woman her name so that she could thank her for her kindness and simple suggestion.

There were many ups and downs in Sally's business as it grew. Some things she got right and many others she had to correct and learn from. The team wrote down who was responsible for which task, so that everyone knew where to go if they had questions. Communication between different teammates improved and the business started to feel less disordered and confused. Sally made a point of spending more time with her customers, understanding what was going well and what could be improved on. She started to see her friends again and get home in time to see her husband and children. It was hard for her not to feel guilty about time spent away from her business, but she noticed that she often had her best ideas and solutions to problems when she was outside walking, chatting with friends or simply sitting on the bench by the river with her eyes closed, feeling the sun on her face.

She was amazed at how often her team would remind her to focus on what she was good at. Sometimes she would wonder how it was possible that she got to do all the things that she loved and was good at and none of the things that had so overwhelmed her previously. But then she would look at her team, all doing what each of them wanted to do and thriving as the company grew. And any time Sally felt herself feeling stuck or overwhelmed, she remembered the woman's advice: ask *who* rather than *how*.

Introduction

'Be yourself. Everyone else is taken.'
— Oscar Wilde, Irish poet and playwright

This book is written for Sally and people like her: people who want to take their business to the next level but aren't sure how. People who feel that their business is taking over their life, who want to do more and do better. Entrepreneurs who want to solve problems and have a positive impact on the customers and communities they serve.

As well as being exhilarating, absorbing and fulfilling, it can be really tough to start, manage and grow a business. It requires you to do things you've never tried before, engage with people you might not normally talk to and take on responsibility that may feel heavy and unwieldy on your shoulders.

There's a real difference between being self-employed and building a business. Many people who start businesses swap a job working for someone else with one working for themselves. Perhaps they want to do things their way, without anyone telling them what to do, or maybe they want more flexibility or the ability to work with multiple clients. The point is that they're still *doing*. Whatever it is that they're good at, they keep doing it, but this time on a freelance basis or for several clients. Building a business involves stepping away from what you're good at, at least for a time, and embracing a whole load of things that you never, ever thought you'd get involved in and that are likely to push you way outside your comfort zone. You may still be involved in the core delivery of the product or service, but that 'delivery hat' will be very different from the one you need to wear to build a business. Michael Gerber, author of *The E-Myth Revisited* (HarperCollins, 2009), puts it bluntly: 'If your business depends on you, you don't own a business – you have a job. And it's the worst job in the world because you're working for a lunatic!' Whether that's true for you or not, the decision of whether or not to build a business is not one to take lightly. The self-employed option suits many perfectly.

If you're feeling overwhelmed by your business and want to get up and out of the day-to-day running of it, then this is the book for you. If you're spread too thin and wishing your team would step up, then this book will show you the way. If you feel that you need some structure in your life and your business, then you're in the right place. The important thing is to build a business that works for you.

A lot has been written on getting clear about why we do what we do. Simon Sinek, the author of *Start with Why: How Great Leaders Inspire Everyone to Take Action* (Penguin, 2011), says that, 'People don't buy what you do, they buy why you do it.' If you're feeling overwhelmed by your business, knowing *why* you do what you do may help you stay motivated but it's unlikely to get you out of the hole. If you're struggling to manage a team of people who aren't communicating and who don't trust each other, knowing *why* might help you rally the troops but it probably won't fix the underlying issues.

Introducing the REAL model®

I've spent many years getting things done. I've worked with many leaders, of companies large and small, who had a clear idea of *what* they wanted to achieve and looked to me to figure out *how* to achieve it. There is enormous power in different kinds of people working together to achieve great things. I understand what makes these types of business partnerships work and I want to share that with you.

In my experience, trying to think about *what* and *how* at the same time, which is what many entrepreneurs are trying to do, can be exhausting and overwhelming. Many people begin to doubt themselves and feel guilty about all of their 'weaknesses'. I want to help you play to your strengths and focus on what you're good at and what puts you in your particular zone or flow. I want to get you thinking about energy, what leaves you feeling drained and exhausted and what makes you feel you can keep going forever.

Over the years, I've noticed that successful entrepreneurs have certain things in common. They are resilient, energised, accountable leaders. I've developed a model which encompasses these qualities and applies them to entrepreneurs and their businesses. I use it to help people build and grow businesses that meet their needs and those of their customers and communities. I call it the REAL model® because it addresses real problems that show up in businesses as they scale. It's a practical model which can be applied to your business wherever you are in your journey, whatever your industry or type of business and whatever it is that's causing you to feel stuck, overwhelmed or in need of support.

The REAL model® is divided into four pillars – Resilience, Energy, Accountability and Leadership – which make up the core of any business. It starts with looking after yourself, because if you're not OK then you can't really take care of your team, customers or business. The model then tackles how to play to your strengths and build a strong team around you. By understanding how you're wired and where you get your energy from, you can attract the right people to you. Once you have these people around you, you can start thinking about accountability, structure and process in order to grow. Building the delivery engine and sharing the management load are the keys to scaling any business. The final piece of the model looks at your role as a leader and how it evolves and changes as your business grows. It invites you to think about how you show up every day.

How to use this book

This book is all about how to focus on the fundamentals of running a growing business without it overwhelming you. It will help you understand who you need around you to make your business dreams a reality.

This book uses my REAL model® as its foundation. Think of resilience as the heart of your business, energy as its life blood, accountability as the skeleton that gives it structure, and leadership as its driving force. The aim is for you to quickly and easily find the areas of the model that will help you to see more clearly, unlock what is blocking you and your business and move towards your goals.

Each chapter is set out so that you can quickly find what you need – from tools and tips to case studies and mistakes to avoid. At the end of the book is a Further Reading section structured in the same way. It includes links to resources should you want to dig deeper into any topic.

I encourage you to read through all four pillars of the REAL model®. But if you need help now and want to solve a specific problem, here's my guide to where to dive in first. Some of these problems may resonate with you, others you may recognise from what your team or people around you are saying.

Head straight to the Resilience section if you or others are noticing any of these problems:

- Loneliness or isolation

- Loss of perspective

- Working too hard/close to burnout

- Feeling out of your comfort zone

- Lots of mistakes being made

- Blame culture setting in

- Organisation feeling unstable

- Market/competition moving too fast

- Procrastination

The Energy section is where to start if any of these problems seem familiar:

- Doing everything yourself (especially things that drain you)

- Disappointment with business partner

- Need to know and understand everything

- Can't find or keep good people

- Breakdown in trust and communication

- High staff turnover

- Pressure on your prices

- Too much competition
- Not enough customers

If you feel that you need a bit more structure in your business then Accountability is where to start. Look out for these problems:

- People unclear who is working on what
- Messy organisation chart/overlapping roles
- Inconsistent delivery to customer
- Spread too thin/all roads still leading to you
- Struggling to trust and let go
- Wishing your senior team would step up
- Decision-making not clear
- Lots of surprises
- Business feels out of control

If any of these problems resonate with you, then start with the Leadership section:

- Everyone pulling in different directions
- Frequent change of focus
- Confused by conflicting inputs
- Hiring people who don't work out
- Conflict and cliques

- A lot of work but no team spirit

- Lack of momentum

- Unclear priorities

- Constant firefighting

Whether you read through it systematically or dive in to particular chapters, this book will enable you to get clear about how to take your business forward. It may be a tool or case study that resonates with you, or reading about common mistakes that business owners make. However you approach this book, you'll come away with a different way of looking at your business.

But more than that, by the end of this book, you'll know what it means to be a real entrepreneur – a resilient, energised, accountable leader. Throughout this book I'll emphasise what I believe to be the fundamental truths of any business – however long it has been trading and whatever its size, location or industry:

- Business is a team sport – you don't need to know it all and you don't have to do it all

- Be where you are in the journey – it's not a race

- Play to your strengths and speak your truth

- Asking for help is the most important thing you can do

My fervent hope is that through reading this book, you will rediscover what made you want to be an entrepreneur. My mission is to help you play to your strengths while building a strong team and growing a business that works for you.

Let's get started.

Interviews and case studies

Many people gave generously of their valuable time to offer me insights and flavour for this book. Some are named in this book and others chose to remain anonymous. During my interviews, I asked each person what advice they would give to other entrepreneurs – what they had learned along the way that might be valuable to others.

AnyGood?

AnyGood? is a crowdsourced talent platform – a curated and diverse network of professionals who recommend other professionals for roles. The company was formed in 2015. I interviewed co-founder and Chief Executive Officer (CEO) Juliet Eccleston and co-founder and Chief Operating Officer (COO) Carl Webber in September 2017. Juliet told me that building a team of people you trust is critical to ensuring you can endure the stressful moments that come with building a business. Carl agreed. He explained that you have to be prepared for the weight of making decisions with no one but each other to rely on.

The Dots

The Dots is a diverse community of 'no-collar' professionals that includes creators, entrepreneurs and freelancers. The platform was launched in 2014. I interviewed founder and CEO Pip Jamieson and Chief Operating and Financial Officer John Down in September 2017. Pip told me that it's all about the people. 'Don't try to do it all. You just can't and actually it will definitely kill you and be bad for business as well. Put brilliant people around you.' John added, 'It's easy to get lost in your commercial, legal, financial, regulatory and HR responsibilities. So work out what the thresholds are at which commercial, legal or financial issues become *material* to the company. Then use these thresholds to surface the core issues and focus on those.'

Hire Hand

Hire Hand is an on-demand platform for small food businesses that fills front- and back-of-house shifts on a regular or last-minute basis. It was launched in 2015. I interviewed Scott Erwin, founder and CEO, in October 2017. Scott believes that many founders burn themselves out because they feel that they have to be a 'constant cheerleader', which isn't scalable. 'Your business is only scalable at that moment when you actually realise that it's happening without you.'

Landbay

Landbay is a specialist marketplace lending platform for prime residential buy-to-let mortgages. Founded in 2014, it combines market expertise with technological innovation to benefit both investors and landlords. I interviewed co-founder and CEO John Goodall and COO Julian Cork in September 2017. John told me that it's hard for founders to know when and what to let go of. His advice to other entrepreneurs is to 'know what you're good at and to be honest about it'.

LawBite

LawBite is a complete solution for businesses that need access to affordable, understandable and accessible law. The company was formed in 2011. I interviewed CEO and chairman Clive Rich and COO Richard Royce in October 2017. Both Clive and Richard told me they lean on people more than resources. Clive said, 'There's always help. You haven't always got the experience and there are challenges that I can't see beyond. So I tend to talk to people. It's a good habit.'

Whyte & Co

Whyte & Co is a progressive civil enforcement company. It was established in 1981. I interviewed husband-and-wife-team Paul and Julia Whyte in September 2017. They told me that it's important to learn which battles to fight to ensure that momentum remains in the business.

Tools, exercises and lists

Throughout this book, I've included tools, exercises and lists to help you implement the things we discuss. Here's where to find them:

Creating a healthy routine	Chapter 1
The list tool	Chapter 1
Getting the right help	Chapter 2
Continuous improvement tool	Chapter 2
Embracing mistakes tool	Chapter 2
Overcoming decision fatigue	Chapter 3
Overcoming procrastination	Chapter 3
Annual inventory tool	Chapter 3
Partnership mindset	Chapter 4
Partnership conversation tool	Chapter 4
People finder tool	Chapter 5

PART ONE

R IS FOR RESILIENCE

Starting, running and growing a business is hard. Being an entrepreneur can feel like being in a car with no brakes on an icy road or being blindfolded and spun round before being asked to pin the tail on the donkey. It can be overwhelming, infuriating and exhilarating all at the same time. The ability to get back up when you've been knocked down is an important trait for anyone to develop, but for entrepreneurs it's vital. Resilience is at the heart of the REAL model® because giving yourself what you need is just as important as doing the right things for your business.

If you're feeling lonely or isolated, worried you might be losing perspective, or close to burning out, then this section is where to start. Feeling out of your comfort zone is a common enough experience for many entrepreneurs, but if you and your team keep repeating the same mistakes, and spreading blame around, this section will help you gain perspective and give you some ways to improve the resilience of your business. If there's a lot of chaos in your business and the market you operate in, it can become all too easy to procrastinate, convincing yourself that no decision is better than taking an action that may not be 'right' for your business. This section will help you focus not just on your own resilience but also on that of the business you're building.

Resilience starts with a willingness and ability to ask for help. If you can combine that with an openness to learning from mistakes and the flexibility to adapt to what the world throws at you, you and your business have a good chance of being successful.

CHAPTER ONE

Support

'You are never strong enough that you don't need help.'
— Cesar Chavez, American labour leader and civil
  rights activist

There's no doubt that running a business is challenging, but we don't always question whether it needs to be quite so difficult. The industrial-age work ethic of the post-war generation has filtered down into many of the baby boomers and their children – the idea that nothing worth having comes easily, that we need to lead by example and work harder and longer than anyone else. In theory, running a business gives us the freedom to be our own boss, freedom to manage our time and do what we want. And in return for this 'freedom' we accept that it's difficult without necessarily asking ourselves if there's another way.

Some people approach running a business as if it were a code to crack. 'I'll figure it out,' they tell themselves.

'There must be an answer – I'm so close.' They work harder and harder, convinced that the solution is just around the next corner. When we do this, we risk losing perspective and sacrificing more than we ever planned to. The pressure on our finances, our families and our health can be considerable. It's easy to look at other people and think that they have all the answers. The world of the entrepreneur has its fair share of bravado and showmanship, which can often stop people from asking questions or being honest about how they're doing. It's not uncommon for people to feel guilty and blame themselves for every problem that their business encounters. Some even convince themselves that they must be stupid for not being able to make their business a success. Being your own boss and setting your own agenda can be a wonderful freedom, but many entrepreneurs burn themselves out due to a lack of support and perspective.

It's common to get completely consumed by your business, so close to every twist and turn. Maybe your friends and family don't understand what you do or how hard it is. You may find yourself slipping more and more into a lonely and isolated place, unable to see your situation clearly. It's not unusual for entrepreneurs to feel overwhelmed by some kind of fear, whether it be fear of failure or rejection, fear of not being good enough or even fear of success.

We can end up existing in a bubble of our own thoughts. We each have a picture inside our head of who we think we are. Our brain looks for evidence to support that picture, however real or imagined it might be. Especially when things are tough, we can begin to doubt ourselves, and if left unchallenged, the 'reality' that we see becomes distorted.

Some people get stuck in a 'knowledge/skills trap', convinced that only people with deep industry knowledge can manage anything in their field. It's true that industry experience can be hugely beneficial when looking for solutions or making sure that you don't reinvent the wheel. But it's also true that it takes a combination of skills and experience to manage a business and we all need help from people who bring different things to the table. Many entrepreneurs have deep roots and huge credibility in their chosen industry but may not have experience managing people or structuring a business as it grows. They may not have much experience working with anybody who isn't like them. For example, a good designer may instinctively understand how best to work with other designers and have excellent insights into what their customers really want, but they may have little or no understanding of how to manage or work with operational people.

Being an entrepreneur means tackling things you never thought you would, being confronted by tasks and problems you didn't even know existed. You may have spent years specialising in something and then suddenly you're forced to become a generalist overnight, learning how to draw up contracts, set up systems, manage people and a million and one other things besides.

Many people find asking for help difficult. Often, our instinct is to try and figure everything out ourselves. Perhaps we feel that asking for help makes us weak. Maybe we're worried about losing control or having to share. We get so used to doing everything ourselves that it can be hard to let go.

It's also not always easy to be honest about how we're feeling and how our business is really doing. Some of the reactions to Elon Musk's frank admission of burn-out could make even the bravest entrepreneur pause. Sections of the media reacted negatively, Tesla's stock took a hit and people took it upon themselves to denounce his 'self-obsession' (see Further Reading for more details).

With a lack of support, we risk becoming overwhelmed and making poor decisions. Becoming a real entrepreneur means accepting that we cannot do it all alone. It means asking for and accepting help.

Support – Look after yourself

Support starts with looking after yourself, finding what works for you, but it also involves asking for help. This will mean different things to each and every person but, as Arianna Huffington said in her open letter to Elon Musk (see Further Reading), 'This is not about working hard – of course you're always going to work hard. It's about working in a way that allows you to make your best decisions.'

In this chapter, we'll look at how to create a healthy routine, the importance of environment and how to get the help and support that you and your business need.

The power of a healthy routine

Everybody's daily, weekly and monthly routines are different. Many people prefer to get everything clear at the end of each day, so that they can start the next one feeling clear and in control. Many others protect the first hour of the morning at all costs, as they know they'll be at their most creative before the juggling of the day starts. Others know that looking at their phone and, especially, reading email first thing in the morning can make them much less productive. This is because every email, every alert on your phone, every decision that you know you'll have to make, opens up a new 'loop' in your brain which then starts working in your subconscious. So even if you think you're totally focused on what you're doing, the more 'loops' you have running, the more difficult it will be to concentrate.

Many people choose to segment their day or week into different types of activity to help their brain focus and increase efficiency. I would encourage you to try different things until you find what works for you. Nicolas Cole, founder of Digital Press, wrote an article about burnout and how to avoid it (see Further Reading). By 'burnout' he doesn't mean just

41

the big scary events that everyone hears about, but all those times when your brain feels overloaded and you suddenly 'don't want to do anything at all'. He believes that it is the transition between activities rather than the activities themselves that exhausts us and makes us feel stretched too thin. His solution is to give yourself some 'input' between activities – read for a few moments, go for a short walk, just sit and reflect. These inputs, Cole argues, refresh our minds and get us ready for the next activity. I've been amazed at the impact just taking a few moments 'away' can have on my mental state, at the power of getting up and walking around the block or simply making a cup of tea without thinking about anything else.

Being disciplined and kind to yourself is essential – otherwise, burnout and stress are constant threats. Don't just get into the habit of working ridiculous hours. It may have impressed your boss back in the day, but does anybody actually care anymore? Building a business is hard work, but don't make it harder by forming bad habits, such as never seeing your friends and family or having no balance in your life. Decide in the morning what time you're going to finish your day and stick to it wherever possible. If you have to run over, do it consciously and deliberately, and in the full knowledge of the decision you're making. Time management may be an illusion, but let's make sure that we don't end up giving time control over us.

Everybody is different, and so the blend and balance will be different for each person. It's worth taking the time to figure out what's going to work for you. Instead of telling yourself that you *should* be doing certain things, try asking, 'What would work in my life?'

Creating a healthy routine

Looking after yourself means attending to your physical as well as mental health. Here are the elements of a healthy routine that are important to me. I try to live by these regardless of what's going on in my life. You will no doubt want to add to or delete from this list to create a routine that suits you and your lifestyle.

Eat a healthy and balanced diet

This will be different for each person, so try and listen to what your body is telling you. Be kind to yourself. If you're anything like me, you'll have tried your fair share of fad diets or got all enthusiastic about a particular food or gadget only to have it fall by the wayside when things get tough or life gets in the way. When it comes to what you eat, make it easy to stick to and ensure that it fits into your life.

Exercise regularly

You don't have to pound the pavements or strain under heavy weights. A brisk walk once a day will do wonders for your mental and physical health. Stretching or yoga is a great way to start and end the day and will help you stay healthy.

Have a daily routine that works for you

There are many advocates of having a regular morning routine, and I can definitely attest to the benefits of meditation and journaling in terms of keeping me calm and grounded. I find it helpful to also have an evening routine to prepare my body and mind for bed. Committing to a routine upfront also reduces the likelihood that tiredness or stress will make you forget to or simply not do the things you know have a positive impact on you.

Sleep

The importance of a good night's sleep is often underestimated in terms of its impact on your physical and mental health. Reducing your exposure to blue light in the evenings, reducing the amount of liquid you drink before bed and ensuring that light and sound are blocked out are all steps you can take that will improve your sleep.

Build in regular time to reflect and recharge

This is a really hard one for many people, including me. I've made a real effort to plan pauses in my day and week to allow for reflection and recharge my batteries. Deep breathing is known to have a positive impact on our physical and mental health, but I believe that a different kind of breathing – taking pauses in your day, week, month – can be just as life-changing.

Make space in your life for things that are important to you

This is about ensuring that your priorities are reflected in how you choose to spend your time. We all have the same twenty-four hours in a day. I spent years giving myself a hard time for working too hard. The guilt and stress built up over a long period of time. The way I resolve this in my head is to do a deal with myself. If I eat properly, exercise regularly and take better care of myself then we can stop talking about how hard I work. The first time I did this, something clicked in my head. I couldn't believe that it was that simple, and it still works for me today.

Have a system to get things out of your head

Many people really struggle with having too much to 'carry' in their heads. Feeling overwhelmed and having too many things to remember can impact your sleep and mental health in a major way.

In the Further Reading section of this book, you'll find links to several books and articles on nutrition, exercise, sleep and reflection written by people far more quali-fied than I am. I can, however, share with you the tool that I use to help me get things out of my head.

This tool can be used to keep you feeling organised and on top of things throughout the day. It can also help you avoid waking up in the night with too many things running around your head. This simple tool really helps me stay focused, and I try to end each day feeling organised and in control and knowing what I'm facing the next day.

The list tool

1. **Big List** – Have a list of everything you want to get done – add things to it whenever they occur to you. Some people use colour-coding, some use technology. Some have several lists, others one big, long list. I just use the Notes app on my phone. Whatever works for you. The important thing is to have a list that you can access most of the time (including if you wake in the night with your head full). Getting things out of your head should make you feel lighter and might even help you get back to sleep.

2. **Small List** – Every evening (or morning if you prefer), make a list of the things you want to achieve the next/that day. Limit yourself to a handful (some will stick to a top three), put them in order of priority and be realistic about the time requirements. Some people put these on a sticky note, some on a separate list. I put them at the top of my long list, separated out from the rest with a space.

3. **During the day** – Each day, work through your Small List in the order that you decided the night before or that morning. Don't deviate or let yourself get distracted. When new things come into your head (or ping up on your phone), add them to the Big List to be considered later. Trust your judgement and don't second-guess yourself. When you feel yourself getting overwhelmed, focus on the Small List. If you start procrastinating, move on to the next item on the Small List.

4. **End of day** – At the end of the day (or first thing the next morning), add any unfinished items to the Big List. Don't give yourself a hard time. Review your Big List (or at least the most recently added items) and write your Small List for the next/coming day. Remind yourself of the progress you've made and show yourself the Small List for the next/coming day. Ask yourself why you procrastinated over some tasks and decide if there's something you could do to help yourself, some way of breaking them down or someone who could help you complete them.

5. **Weekly** – Review your whole Big List and organise it. I have mine in sections which move around depending on what I'm focusing on. This is your time to think about priorities and goals, but I find that separating the decision-making from the actual doing can be really helpful.

Of course, creating a healthy routine isn't just important for you as the business owner – it's also critical to think about for your business. In subsequent chapters we'll look at having a rhythm in how you manage your business, but thinking about what your business needs to stay healthy is a great way to build up its resilience.

Environment

Breakthroughs often follow breakdowns. When we feel confused, stuck and frustrated, often the quickest way to get to a breakthrough is to change our environment. This why we often have our best ideas when we're away from our regular workspace, in the shower or out for a walk. This is why going on a retreat, doing some physical activity or simply taking a break can have such a powerful impact on our mindset.

In his book *Willpower Doesn't Work: Discover the Hidden Keys to Success* (Piatkus, 2018), Benjamin Hardy argues that our environment has a powerful impact on the way we operate and make decisions. He believes that it's often too stimulating and compulsive to be 'tuned out' by sheer grit and determination. He advises setting up our environment to support and facilitate what we need. This means having a clean and tidy desk to help us feel organised. It means avoiding situations or environments which we know we'll find distracting. And it may even mean finding different spaces to do different kinds of activities – for example, a particular environment that makes you feel creative or inspired, and a different space that encourages you to get on with things you find challenging. If you want to get more active, make it easier by being around people who are active and by planning exercise or movement into your day. We're all a product of our environments, so if we want to make changes in our lives, we need to pay attention to the environments in which we operate.

Where do you go to be creative or to connect with people? What's your ideal place for reflection and feeling grounded? And where's the best place for you to just get things done?

Environment isn't just about you as an individual. The environment of your business is also important.

What's the space like that your people work in? What opportunities do your team have to mix things up? Is your business able to move around and function in different environments?

Getting help

The next step in looking after ourselves is to surround ourselves with people who will support, inspire, challenge and encourage us. As entrepreneurs, we have more choice than most about who we spend time with – it's important to gain perspective to avoid being in a bubble of our own thoughts. Here are a few options.

A **coach** will work with you to uncover your own solutions to issues you're facing. They will challenge the picture you have of yourself and the stories you tell yourself, to help you get clear about your goals and how to achieve them and deal with whatever is standing in your way or holding you back.

A **mentor** will usually have experience in your industry or type of business and can give you advice and guidance as well as perspective on your business, your team, your customers and your competitors. They will also act as a sounding board when you want to talk through issues.

Business **advisors** can be crucial assets to your business, bringing specific industry or sector knowledge and expertise to the table and offering you objective and robust challenge. As you grow your business, especially if you raise money from investors, you'll need to formalise your governance structures (we'll cover this in the Accountability chapter).

A strong and active **board** is something that many owners underestimate the value of. Successful entrepreneurs will often acknowledge the positive impact on the development of their companies of rigorous governance processes and the challenging accountability of their board.

Joining a **mastermind**, support or accountability group is an opportunity to meet with like-minded people. This is a great way to get perspective and realise that you're not alone – others have been, and are, where you are now – and that things can change. Share stories and learn from each other – the support you receive and give will be invaluable.

One of the underestimated advantages of going through rigorous fundraising rounds is the challenge you get to your business model. If you take on the right **investors** then they can become valuable resources to challenge and support you, introduce you to people you need to meet and help you stay on track.

Getting the right help

So, which do you choose and how do you find the right help and support for you?

1. Be clear about what outcomes you are looking for and what you are prepared to put in in terms of time and energy. *What am I trying to achieve? What do I feel is missing?*

2. Do your research – ask colleagues and peers for recommendations, look online. *Who has been recommended to me? What have I found online?*

3. Arrange a call with the person or people you're looking to work with. *What questions do I have? How will I know if the person or organisation is right for me?*

4. Get clear about what kind of support you are looking for. *What am I looking for in terms of support? Is it a person, a group or several different people?*

As a real entrepreneur, I recommend you try a blended approach, possibly a combination of individual coaching or mentoring plus attending a mastermind group like the one that I run.

I also recommend having specific advisors to support on areas of importance or where you feel that your knowledge or experience is lacking.

For individual team members, consider mentoring or buddying up – having someone to talk with who isn't directly involved in the day-to-day can encourage people to open up and explore different options.

Sharing the load

I mentioned earlier that most entrepreneurs have to become generalists when they start out in business and yet that feeling of having to do and know everything can be completely overwhelming. In my view, the only way to grow your business and get back in touch with what you love and are good at is to share the load as soon as you can. In the Energy chapter of this book, we'll explore how to find the right kind of people to complement you and your skills, experience and preferences, but it's a critical part of looking after yourself to accept that you cannot and should not try to carry it all yourself. For many of us, asking for help is one of the hardest things we'll ever have to do, but it's essential. Having help and support gives us confidence, as does knowing that we have people around us who will challenge and help us see when we're veering off track. Your people are likely to follow your lead, so you need to ensure that you're being honest with yourself and asking for the help and support you need.

Support – Top three takeaways

1. Find a routine that works for you

2. Ask for help

3. Surround yourself with people who inspire and lift you up

CHAPTER TWO

Learning

'Life can only be understood backwards, but it must be lived forwards.'

— Søren Kierkegaard, Danish philosopher

In many businesses, mistakes are whispered about, stigmatised as defects and associated with embarrassment or even fear. Blame becomes an automatic response and taking responsibility is simply not an option. In these organisations there tends to be a lack of clarity about who is responsible for what and a lack of commitment to excellence.

Not only do these organisations not prioritise initiative or learning, they don't tend to celebrate their successes. They're too busy delivering for their customers, moving on to the next project as soon as they've finished the current one and firefighting the myriad actions, issues and decisions required every day. These businesses have a high tolerance for mediocre people and can become toxic places to work – they repeat mistakes over and over, lose customers and team members and ultimately risk stagnation or even closure.

Running a small business can feel like walking a tightrope. The gap between not enough and too many customers can be wafer thin and yet make all the difference. One minute you're worrying that you've hired too many people, and the next it's all hands to the pump to deliver. However hard you try, mistakes are a fact of life – we all make them and so do the businesses that we run and the people who work in them. Many entrepreneurs will tell you that mistakes are unavoidable, and still customers expect a predictable and consistent service every time they deal with you.

Many of you will be familiar with the concept of the comfort zone – that place where we feel safe, things are recognisable, we know where we are and what we're doing. As entrepreneurs we don't necessarily spend a lot of time here. We tend to like to push the boundaries and try out new things. We want to grow, take on more customers, create new products and make more money.

Beyond the comfort zone is the growth zone, and it exists for organisations as well as people. This is where questions get asked, where learning and progression happens, but also where there's increased risk and mistakes are more likely. This is where many entrepreneurs feel comfortable on a personal level – they're pushing themselves and moving forward. But in organisational terms, it can be difficult for many entrepreneurs to accept the level of uncertainty that comes from other people taking risks with their business, trying new things and learning from mistakes. The urge to jump in and save the day can be overwhelming, which means that knowledge and experience stay with the entrepreneur and mistakes by others keep happening.

It's all about balance, though. There's a shock zone beyond the growth zone, where it all gets too much and our brain starts shutting down to protect us. For an organisation this can equate to parts of the business going into meltdown, systems not working, orders not being delivered and conflicts rising to the surface.

From a learning perspective for individuals as well as organisations, the age-old saying 'The comfort zone is a beautiful place, but nothing ever grows there' continues to ring true. To get the best out of ourselves and our teams, we need to push outside of that space where everything is easy, the status quo, the easy path. By allowing people to explore the art of the possible, learning and improvements can be made.

Learning – Embrace mistakes

An organisation's ability to learn sets it apart from its competitors and makes it more resilient. Customers expect and deserve consistent, reliable and high-quality delivery of your products and services every single time they do business with you – and that doesn't happen without a lot of hard work. Many of us have a challenging relationship with feedback and 'failure'. As students, we sat exams and generally received a pass (good) or fail (bad) mark. But business doesn't really work like that. Sometimes we get lucky, but it's usually by trying things out that we learn what our customers want and how best to deliver it to them. It helps not to take things personally – what you do is not who you are! In this chapter, we'll look at how to create a culture of learning and the importance of celebrating success.

Creating a culture of learning

Learning, as with so many things, starts from the top. The most successful entrepreneurs are those who are constantly learning. As Pip Jamieson of The Dots told me, 'You have to adopt that appetite to always be challenging how you're doing things. Always be learning new things.'

It's vital to create a culture of learning in your business. Rather than punishing failure, try to treat it as part of the learning process. Peter Senge, author of *The Fifth Discipline: The Art and Practice of the Learning Organization* (Cornerstone Digital, 2010), describes a learning organisation as 'a group of people working together collectively to enhance their capabilities to create results they really care about'. In practical terms, this means embracing mistakes, even celebrating them. It means taking time to think about what you would do differently next time and updating your systems and processes accordingly. In my view, all mistakes are positive as long as you don't make the same mistake twice. The only way to build consistency is to get mistakes out in the open so that you can learn from them. This means rewarding initiative even when things don't work out quite as planned.

One of the biggest inhibitors to learning is to say 'I know that', which is a way for our brains to shut off and move on. If you know it but don't do it then you don't really know it. This is as true for teams and organisations as it is for individuals. Before concluding that you know something, ask yourself if that knowledge is contained within your business or only in your head. Is it something that you and your business actually do, or simply something that you know?

Here are two tools to help you – Continuous improvement and Embracing mistakes.

Continuous improvement tool

At the end of every meeting, project, campaign or event, ask each member of your team to answer three simple questions:

1. What would we score the meeting, project, campaign or event out of ten?

2. What did we do well?

3. What would we do differently next time?

This process keeps you moving forward and avoids negativity.

Embracing mistakes tool

This tool is to be used for a more systematic look at your business and its ability to learn. It can be used to uncover mistakes and start to create a culture of learning. I suggest using it quarterly and, as your business grows, make it part of each new team or function that forms. For example, if you're building a sales or tech team, you could hold a regular review with the team to look at what's gone well and what could be improved.

1. **Identify** – The first step in embracing mistakes is to identify them. Look at process breakdowns or overlapping tasks where more than one person was trying to do the same thing, perhaps from

a different angle. All customer complaints must be looked at carefully to understand what went wrong and why, and how they can be prevented from happening again (after you've responded to the customer who complained of course). *What can be identified as a mistake? What could the business or team have done better?*

2. **Embrace** – Before you go about fixing things, it's a good idea to recognise the value of finding the mistake. To create a culture of openness and trust, you need to make it a *positive thing* to identify mistakes. *Why is it a good thing to have found or recognised the mistake? Who gets the credit for openness and honesty? How can we reward them?*

3. **Record** – Making a record of each mistake increases awareness and makes it less likely to reoccur. *What exactly happened or didn't happen?*

4. **Diagnose** – This is where you work out what went wrong. It's essential that this step is not used as an excuse to blame but instead approached as an opportunity to learn. Encourage constructive feedback and challenge. *Why did this mistake occur? What process broke down? What was missed?*

5. **Learn** – This is the step where you look at what can be learned from the mistake. *What can be done differently next time? Who needs support? What needs to change? What can be improved?*

6. **Prevent** – The holy grail of a learning organisation. This is where the team gets to improve how they

do things and ensure that the same mistake is not repeated. *How can this be stopped from happening next time?*

It takes time and effort to conduct these reviews, but Matthew Syed, author of *Black Box Thinking: The Surprising Truth About Success* (John Murray, 2015), argues that success is strongly linked to how we react to failure. He contrasts how the airline industry and the healthcare industry deal with failure. In the aviation industry, every plane is fitted with a black box, which records the conversations and sounds in the cockpit. Every time there's an accident, the black box is analysed and the reason for the accident investigated. Near misses are also recorded so that lessons can be learned and failures eliminated. The industry has worked hard to become open and honest about mistakes, an approach which starkly contrasts with that of the healthcare industry, where cases of clinical negligence are on the rise. It still tends to hide the truth behind 'technical errors' and 'complications'. It's not the only industry to suffer from a 'blame culture', where everything is someone else's fault and people are reluctant to accept responsibility, but it's a good example of what happens when organisations are reluctant to take responsibility and really learn from their mistakes.

As a real entrepreneur, it's up to you to lead from the top. Acknowledge mistakes and use them as an opportunity for everyone to learn. Most people are more productive and likely to stay in a business where instead of pointing the finger of blame people are encouraged to admit their mistakes and take responsibility for ensuring that they aren't repeated.

Celebrating success

Business can be a struggle, and many of the wins we achieve as entrepreneurs are a result of time, effort and dedication from our teams. It's important to celebrate all that effort if you want your team to stay engaged and productive. In her book *Your Best Year Yet: Make the Next 12 Months your Best Ever!* (HarperElement, 2012), Jinny Ditzler talks about a cycle of productivity. This looks like a traditional project cycle in three phases starting with the idea and initiation phase, moving into action and progress, and ending with the completion phase. But according to Ditzler, there needs to be a fourth phase, which she calls 'acknowledge and celebrate'. This is where she believes the magic happens but it's often missed by busy teams and organisations. To quote Ditzler: 'Too many of us simply go straight from the end of the third segment (completion) back to the starting line without taking a pause for acknowledgment... Our eye is always on what's next or what hasn't been completed.' She argues that without the fourth step, we'll quickly stop feeling satisfied and motivation will dip. If all we focus on is speed and efficiency, we'll become disengaged and disconnected. Teresa Amabile and Steven Kramer, authors of *The Progress Principle: Using Small Wins to Ignite Joy,*

Engagement and Creativity at Work (Harvard Business Review Press, 2011), argue that we're less productive when we don't take time to recharge and reflect and when we don't acknowledge and celebrate our successes. In his book *Oversubscribed: How to Get People Lining Up to Do Business with You* (Capstone, 2015), Daniel Priestley talks about the importance of celebration and innovation. 'You need to hunt down the stories, capture the numbers, interrogate the data – then learn, share, congratulate and reward those involved.'

Pip Jamieson of The Dots told me that her team have twice-weekly work-in-progress meetings so that everyone on the team understands what everyone else is doing. 'At the beginning of the week it's about talking about what you're doing for the rest of the week, and at the end of the week we do thank yous. So everyone thanks another person on the team.' She told me that it was one of the most valuable things that they do as a team, to learn from and recognise each other. I've seen companies who have a gratitude board (either physical or virtual), where they stick up messages of thanks or acknowledgement for other team members. Some use a Slack channel to achieve the same result. The point is to focus on learning and ensure that people feel recognised and acknowledged.

Clive Rich from LawBite holds a management meeting every Monday. 'We set the tone for the week. Everyone puts up on the board their three priorities for the week, what I'm going to work on that is aligned, what we should be thinking about. And then come the beginning of next week, we can review what went well or badly last week, and what we need to do this week.'

Carl Webber from AnyGood? told me that he wants challenge to be the norm as they grow their culture. He talked about wanting the team to be comfortable with having open conversations about issues and learning from them.

My personal favourite lesson about learning comes in the form of a poem written by Portia Nelson, an American singer, songwriter, actress and author, called 'Autobiography in Five Short Chapters'. She talks about falling into the same hole over and over again, managing to find your way out a little more easily each time, until you realise that you don't even need to walk past the hole anymore, let alone fall in it. It's a simple yet powerful way of looking at the cycles of life, those patterns that we seem to repeat again and again until we become conscious of them and decide to make different choices.

This simple poem has been used in many different settings and by many different people, from therapists to authors, singers and motivational speakers. It was even included in a Broadway show. Its powerful message can be applied equally to business and the way individuals and teams deal with success, failure and how to learn.

A culture of learning starts from the top. It's key to the resilience of your organisation and its ability to thrive. Learning and support are also closely linked. As you grow your business, you need to create a culture where asking for help in order to learn is encouraged. Unlearning can sometimes be as important as learning. Things that worked at the start won't necessarily keep working. You'll also need to be open to relearning some things that you'd forgotten or thought no longer worked for you. In the next chapter, we'll look at why flexibility is just as important as learning for a growing business and a developing team.

Learning – Top three takeaways

1. Success is linked to how we deal with failure

2. Mistakes need to be embraced so that we can learn from them

3. Celebrating success increases productivity and motivation

CHAPTER THREE

Flexibility

'The measure of intelligence is the ability to change.'
— Albert Einstein, theoretical physicist

Many markets are evolving quickly, which means that innovation, competitors and automation can leave us feeling completely overwhelmed and our businesses unstable and on edge. People deal with stress, overwork and loss of control in very different ways. Some people internalise and withdraw when something challenging happens. Others prefer to stamp their feet and let the whole world know they aren't happy. When you own a business, your behaviour and the way you choose to respond to things around you has a direct impact on your team, your suppliers and your customers.

The number of decisions we have to make every day can exhaust us and reduce our ability to be flexible. Research into how we make decisions has found that the quality of our decisions erodes throughout the day (see links in Further Reading). Apparently, we have a fixed amount of willpower which can get used up – meaning that our decision-making power is a depletable resource. Just as many of us will succumb to chocolate or crisps after a day full of mentally exhausting healthy decisions, or snap at loved ones at the end of a long and tiring meeting, we're more likely to make bad or hasty management decisions after a day full of hundreds of trivial judgements.

The research shows that the more decisions we have to make, the more mentally tired we'll become until our brains start looking for shortcuts. We either act impulsively or become paralysed with indecision. The impact on our businesses when this happens can be profound. The flexibility and resilience of your people and your organisation will be affected if you're mentally fatigued.

Procrastination and indecision are common examples of lack of flexibility and getting stuck – many of us put off even the most important tasks. It's a very human struggle, and we've been doing it forever. The Ancient Greeks called it *akrasia* – doing one thing when you know you should be doing something else, against your better judgement. It's often 'easier' to get busy with all those smaller, less important things on our list, easier to hope that we'll find the time, the headspace, the right mood to get the big, important stuff done. When we delay, avoid and procrastinate, we decrease our flexibility and increase the likelihood of stress, fear and self-doubt.

The human brain tends to value immediate reward over future potential benefits, which is why we focus on the 'quick and easy'. Although we can conceptually understand that eating well and keeping fit will probably lead to longevity and good health, our immediate issue is that we're hungry now and what we want is a large pizza (or a bottle of wine, or a tub of ice cream). When you're procrastinating as a business owner, best case, opportunities are passing you by – worst case, your business is failing.

For businesses, the pressure to be more and more flexible can be enormous and at times completely contradictory. We want lower and lower prices, but we want business owners to pay their people more and more. We demand flexibility, but we want consistency and good quality.

Flexibility – Adapt and thrive

Flexibility is an essential part of resilience and a vital tool in today's fast-moving world. Dr Joselyn Sellen, an expert in resilience, told me that 'resilience is a flexibility of thinking, behaving and emotions under stress' – essentially, the ability to bounce back after a stressful event. Learning how to control our emotions and mental state helps us to increase our resilience. Recognising how we react in certain situations helps us to increase our self-control and be more considerate of those around us. Looking for solutions rather than focusing on problems is a way of staying in control rather than feeling overwhelmed.

Keeping a record of our strengths and achievements can be a useful way to reflect on what keeps us moving forward, what works and what doesn't. It also reminds us of our ability to cope with stress and recover from challenging events. In this chapter, we'll look at how to overcome decision fatigue and procrastination and how to increase your organisation's flexibility.

Decision fatigue

Entrepreneurs are famous for going with their gut, and it usually serves them well. But when we become overwhelmed and 'stuck', we can start second-guessing ourselves, which usually means that decisions are harder to make. Self-belief can make you more resilient, but sometimes you don't know how you're going to react until you're in the situation. Making a decision and moving forward, even if it means that mistakes happen, is usually better than feeling paralysed with indecision. Here are my top tips for overcoming decision fatigue.

Overcoming decision fatigue

1. Simplify your life – make it as easy as possible to make decisions.

2. Plan daily decisions the night before (for example, what time you're going to start your day, what you're going to wear, whether you're going to the gym or not).

3. Remove the decision by putting it in your diary.

4. Do the most important thing first thing in the morning.

5. Eat well before important decisions (if you can't make them first thing in the morning) but not too much, as it can make you sleepy!

6. Just do it – 5, 4, 3, 2, 1 (see below).

This last one deserves a bit more explanation. In *The 5 Second Rule: Transform Your Life, Work and Confidence with Everyday Courage* (Savio Republic, 2017), author Mel Robbins explains that the brain's job is to protect us and keep us safe, which is why it will try to err on the side of caution. As a result, we can often have what we think is a great idea only to talk ourselves out of it moments later. She suggests a devastatingly simple approach to overcoming the brain's instinctive cautiousness. She argues that most of the time we get things right, and that it's worth the odd mistake just to keep moving forward. She talks about trusting your gut and acting more on instinct. If you agree with that basic premise and are willing to trust that you'll be able to deal with the consequences, whatever they may be, then the rest is easy.

Every time you think of doing something, start a countdown in your head – 5-4-3-2-1 – and before you reach 1, you do the thing, before you have a chance to talk yourself out of it. There is an amazing energy that comes with simply *doing* without too much thought.

Sometimes you just want someone else to give you the answer. Hiring an expert to tell you what to do can be liberating. Make sure you get recommendations from people you trust, and don't fall into the trap of thinking you have to weigh all the facts relating to every decision yourself.

Procrastination

Our ability to be successful will get a huge positive boost if we can get clear about why we put things off and what we can do to help ourselves. Gretchen Rubin, author of *Better Than Before: Mastering the Habits of Our Everyday Lives* (Two Roads, 2015), has a lot of good tips on overcoming procrastination. Here are mine.

Overcoming procrastination

1. Embrace mornings – things usually look better in the morning, so make the decision the night before then just get up and do it.

2. Imagine you're on a deserted island – now that you have all the time in the world, no need to rush or put things off, you can get started.

3. Don't get overwhelmed with too much research – often one choice isn't so different from another. Trust your instinct – action is usually better than indecision.

4. Set it up right – make sure you have what you need – don't let yourself be interrupted.

5. Ask for help – it's amazing how often this can help us get unblocked, so that we can take the first step and move forward.

6. Take one step – just get started. Take the first step. Maybe take one step a day, or maybe only fifteen minutes a day, to get it done.

7. Stop working on other stuff – don't kid yourself that you're just about to get round to it.

It's good practice to pay attention to which things you really dislike doing and what you're putting off. Take notice of *why* you're putting something off and what you're choosing to do instead. Maybe it's time to find someone else to do it? Someone to share the load?

Flexibility in your organisation

A huge amount has been written about the speed of change in today's world. Technology is evolving at breakneck speed. Whole industries are being disrupted and turned on their heads. Physical things that many of us grew up using and seeing around us – music player, telephone, camera, map, address book, calculator, thermometer, diary – have all disappeared into the one device in our pockets. These were things that people used to design, create and build. Things that were bought and sold – companies, industries and jobs – all fundamentally changed in a few short years. The challenge for today's entrepreneur is how to build a sustainable business in such uncertain times.

During the Cold War, the US military developed a model to try to capture the new complexity and dynamism that they were faced with. They named the model VUCA after its four quadrants: volatility, uncertainty, complexity and ambiguity. All of these challenges are as relevant today as they were in the 1980s. Here's a short explanation of each kind of challenge and how best to deal with it as a real entrepreneur.

VUCA

Volatility – The rate of change has increased dramatically in the digital era. Where an average product life cycle was fifteen to twenty years in the pre-digital era, today it's one to five years (and getting shorter). The challenge of volatility is unexpected or unstable events, such as price fluctuations after a natural disaster.

To adapt to volatility, we can look at building slack into our systems and resources. We need to assess the risks carefully to ensure that our investment is proportionate, as these steps can be costly (for example, taking on extra people). A clear vision of the future is essential for the real entrepreneur in volatile times – they must keep their team focused on why they do what they do and how they'll measure success.

Uncertainty – Businesses face unclear situations all the time – we don't always have all the information, but we still need to make decisions. When a competitor launches a new product, we don't know how the market will respond or how we should react.

In responding to uncertainty, we can look at investing in smart ways to capture, analyse and share information. Understanding is required in uncertain times. By bringing the team to a shared mindset and a common understanding of how each person can contribute, the real entrepreneur ensures that everyone keeps pulling in the same direction.

Complexity – With the vast amount of available information, it has become pretty much impossible to be on top of all factors which might influence your decisions. There are just too many to consider – for example, if you're working across multiple legal and regulatory jurisdictions, dealing with many different ways of doing business or managing disparate cultural values.

Our approach here is to build up our resources and potentially bring on board specialists to help us combat complexity. Clarity and simplicity are required. The team will look to you as a real entrepreneur to reinforce priorities and keep everyone focused on serving their customers. Keeping things simple can be a challenge, but having single data sources and clear decision-making processes will go a long way to keeping everyone focused.

Ambiguity – Most of the time, it's not so clear what your world really looks like or what your customers and competitors are doing. Many industries face the risk of disruption, and you may decide to enter new markets or move outside of your core competencies.

Ambiguity requires you to experiment so that you can figure out what works and what doesn't. Make sure your organisation is learning from whatever tests you run. Agility is a key characteristic of a real entrepreneur. Your team will look to you to help them keep moving fast – anticipating change, taking action and moving heaven and earth to meet the needs of your customers.

Flexibility means being able to deal with the various challenges that the VUCA model lays out while keeping your team engaged and your customers happy. You'll need every element of your business to be contributing to ensure you stay on track. I encourage my clients to take a step back and look at their businesses in a different way by using the Annual inventory tool.

You'll need to review some of these items personally, but you can get your team to look at most of them and share their recommendations with you.

Annual inventory tool

1. Maintain a business inventory – a list of every single thing in your business: people, processes, systems and assets.

2. Imagine that everything on this list has been moved outside your business into a metaphorical car park or yard.

3. Systematically work through each item. *Does it add value to your business? Do you choose to keep it?*

4. Justify everything that you bring back, including the people – ask yourself if you would rehire them today.

This tool encourages you to look at each element of your business in a different way. By imagining it outside your business and giving yourself the choice to bring it back 'inside' or not, you may consider things you've been avoiding and make choices that you wouldn't otherwise make. Questioning how you do things and with what resources will help keep you flexible and lean. Remember that not everyone will be able to come all the way with you. As you adapt and grow, some of your team won't be willing or able to keep up, so you may need to let them go. What was right for your business yesterday may not be right for it tomorrow.

As with so many things, flexibility starts at the top. For you as a business owner, it means being open to challenge and new ideas. It means you and your management team are focused on what's right for your team, your customers and your business.

Flexibility also means adapting to the market and what it's telling you. Whyte & Co have had to adapt to new legislation and councils changing what they're willing to outsource. When some councils decided to bring back in-house some of the enforcement activities, Whyte & Co saw an opportunity to provide them with their own custom-built enforcement system, which several councils are now using. They are also active on several industry bodies informing government as it looks to make further changes to legislation.

In a world that's constantly changing, it can be helpful to focus on the things that aren't going to change. What are the constants – the areas that form the foundations of successful businesses? What aspects are difficult to automate and therefore won't see as much change? What are the human elements? Where are the new ideas and creativity coming from in your industry and how can you apply these in your business?

Flexibility – Top three takeaways

1. Willpower and decision-making ability erode during the day

2. Planning and scheduling your decisions will make your life simpler

3. Flexibility is something that can be learned and developed

Bringing Resilience together

Resilience isn't just about your business and how adaptable it may be to the pressures of a changing marketplace, fickle customers and increasing competition. It's also about looking after yourself and ensuring that you have support. Look to eliminate anything that drains your energy – whether it's people who drag you down and make you feel bad, too many open decision 'loops' in your brain or clutter that stops you from getting clear. As you build your business, you'll need to learn to manage your own stress and anxiety, but you'll also increasingly have to think about the team around you. How are people in your team reacting to uncertainty? How well is each person developing, and how well is your business evolving and learning from its mistakes? Each person will have their own levels of comfort and discomfort, which makes it challenging but also exciting when a team is trying to figure out something together. To be a real entrepreneur, you need to focus on balance – life isn't a race. We're all on our own journey towards our own goals.

- What are your key takeaways from the Resilience section?

- What are you going to implement immediately?

- What are you looking at differently now?

PART TWO

E IS FOR ENERGY

It's common for entrepreneurs and leaders of small businesses to feel overwhelmed. The constant firefighting, the feeling out of our comfort zones and the endless list of decisions to be made can make even the most resilient among us feel drained. Energy comes in limited quantities – it grows or diminishes based on what you're doing, where you are and who you're with. It's in the way you manage your company. It can be transferred and shared. It can sustain and move you forward. Energy is a critical element of my REAL model® because it's the life blood of every business. If you can focus on what gives you energy, and what drains it away, then you can really be the best that you can be.

If you're doing everything yourself, finding it frustrating to work with a business partner or constantly feeling that you need to know more, then this section is where to start. If you're ready to share the load but struggle to find and keep good people or if communication is breaking down in your team, then this section will give you insights into how to form the right partnerships and how to improve productivity and trust. If you're constantly worrying about the competition and your prices are regularly under pressure, the impact on your business and your team can be severe. This section will help you get clear about the value you deliver to your customers and how that can feed back into the type of business you're building.

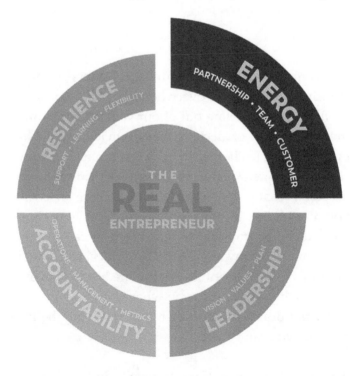

Energy starts with an awareness of your own strengths, weaknesses and preferences – what you can offer and what you need. It comes from the understanding that you can't do everything yourself and in how you form partnerships and build teams of people who complement each other. Understanding your customers, their problems and how you and your team serve them is key to becoming a real entrepreneur.

CHAPTER FOUR

Partnership

'Great CEOs look up and out. Great COOs look down
and in. It's the partnership of their perspectives that
make great companies.'

— Simon Sinek, British-American author and
motivational speaker

Many entrepreneurs don't actually want to be
involved in the day-to-day running of their business but they often don't realise it consciously. They're
usually the brains behind their business – they have
the ideas and the vision, they understand the market
and the opportunities. They start off full of energy,
creativity and ambition. They decide the strategy,
form partnerships, spread the word about their great
products and services, build relationships with investors, customers and partners, and drive growth. This
is often where their strengths lie, but over time, they

get bogged down in minutiae and overwhelmed by firefighting. They don't naturally think about structures and systems. They don't often enjoy all the 'admin', nor are they usually very good at it. Many amazing business owners, who were so good for their business at the start, end up killing it because of their natural desire to 'shake things up' and bring creativity to the table – just at the time when consistency, quality control and stability are required.

When we start out in business, there's usually a long list of things that we don't know. Many entrepreneurs are avid readers; we want to learn and educate ourselves. Luckily there's no shortage of people offering to sell us books, courses, workshops, webinars and seminars. There's a seemingly limitless supply of information for us to absorb on business topics ranging from social media tools to leadership skills, from strategic thinking to operational excellence. For some people, all this information and choice can be overwhelming and confusing. For some, it can also be a source of guilt – all these things that we *should* be doing. The more we read and learn, the longer the list of things we don't have time to do can become. A friend of mine told me that when she started her own business, she felt as if she were surrounded by a million people all giving her 'more jobs to do'.

It's impossible for one person to have all the knowledge, all the answers and all the skills. The risk is that the more things we do, the further we get from the reasons why we started the business in the first place. Often we end up not spending any time doing the bits of the job that we actually love.

Being an entrepreneur can be overwhelming, exhilarating and frustrating, but it can also be lonely. There's no one to tell you what to do, your schedule is your own and every decision rests on your shoulders. As your team grows, the weight of expectation and responsibility can be heavy. As you get busier, it can get harder to ask for help and to think about sharing the management load.

Some entrepreneurs decide from the start that they want to work by themselves, perhaps with a team in support but keeping all management decisions to themselves. This is absolutely their right, but it's unlikely you'll be able to grow a business beyond a handful of people unless you work in partnership with others. It's impossible for one person to oversee sales and marketing, operations and finance, product development and delivery, as well as focusing on business growth.

There are many reasons why entrepreneurs continue to struggle on alone, spread too thin, making all the big decisions and having all roads continue to lead back to them. It usually comes down to time, money, confusion or trust.

Time – Many entrepreneurs wait until they're completely overwhelmed before acknowledging that they need help. You may believe that you don't have time to waste on trying to find the perfect foil for you and your strengths, or maybe you don't see the value of bringing someone else in.

Money – Many entrepreneurs delay bringing in a partner or fellow managers because they don't have the money. It's easy to get into the circular argument of 'I'll bring someone in when I make a few more sales, but I can't make any more sales when I'm so busy'. Don't assume that you know without talking to them how best to structure the reward they'll receive in return for their efforts.

Confusion – Most of us will naturally get drawn to people like ourselves – we recognise them, we like and trust them, and we feel comfortable around them. The problem that many entrepreneurs face is that their natural tendency is to bring in someone like themselves, rather than someone who will complement their strengths, experience and preferences. Even if they do realise that they need someone different, they may have no idea where to start looking for them or what to say when they do find them. They aren't clear about what kind of person they need, even if they accept that they need someone.

Trust – Trust and control are often linked in our minds. When people say that they aren't sure if they could trust another person, they're often expressing a fear of losing control. It can be difficult to imagine sharing control with another person, opening up your finances, wondering if they'll be as committed as you are.

Whether you start off in business alone or with a trusted friend, colleague or even family member, the partnerships you form are likely to come under pressure. You'll probably find that you have different expectations, opinions and ways of working, and even different aspirations for the business. Successful partnerships require a lot of work, but they can take your business to a whole new level.

One of the things that sets real entrepreneurs apart is the way they view collaboration and partnership. The term 'abundance mindset' was coined by Stephen Covey in his best-selling book *The 7 Habits of Highly Effective People: Powerful Lessons in Personal Change* (Rosetta Books, 2013). He defined it as 'a concept in which a person believes there are enough resources and successes to share with others'. The real entrepreneur views customers, suppliers and even competitors as potential partners.

Partnership – Connect and grow

The real entrepreneur may consider many types of partnerships, but I'm going to concentrate on the one where you look at sharing the running of the business with someone else (regardless of capital structure).

In my experience, one of the best ways of defeating that feeling of being stretched too thin is to start the process of sharing the load. But first, we need to get the mindset right. Michael Jordan, former professional basketball player, has been quoted as saying, 'Talent wins games, but teamwork and intelligence win championships.' If you want to go it alone that's your choice, but in that case, you're not a real entrepreneur. In this chapter, we'll look at the partnership mindset, how to identify the right time and the right person, how to start off right and how to make the partnership work for you both and for your business.

Mindset

As outlined at the beginning of the chapter, there are many reasons people give for continuing to do everything themselves. The first step in getting to the right mindset is to overcome these reasons. Here's how to do it.

Partnership mindset

This approach will help you figure out if partnership is right for you. It's for anyone who's considering a partnership but doesn't know where to start. It's also for anyone who doesn't believe that they need to bring in anyone else to run the business with them but is frustrated at having to do everything themselves.

Time – Often it's difficult to even find the time to think about bringing anyone else in. But taking a step back to look at how your business *could* work if you were sharing the load will be worth the effort if it means that your business grows, and you can get your life back. As one of my mentors would say, 'Lack of time is either a lack of people or technology.' Ask yourself, *'What would be the benefit to me and my business of having more time? What would the impact be of focusing on what I do best? What would I do with that extra time? How would it improve my business and my life?'*

Money – Instead of spending one day a week with customers, you could spend three or four. If the business of the future can afford the person you need now, then what you have is a timing issue, rather than a money one. Focus on identifying the right person, rather than on how to pay them. They'll tell you what they want, and together you can figure out how to make it work. Ask yourself, *'How many more customers and how much more revenue could I generate for my business if I only focused on promoting our products and services? How many more customers could I see each week, and how much more money would the business make if I was able to focus on what I'm good at?'*

Confusion – If you're finding it difficult to imagine sharing responsibility with another person, make a list of the business's main activities and imagine splitting them between *what* and *how*. Let's use social media as an example. Imagine one person concentrating on the high-level 'what is our message?' and someone else thinking about 'how do we go about communicating that?'. Once you're clearer about this split, it will be easier for you to see how the two roles might work together. Ask yourself, *'What are the main areas of my business? How would I split them between* what *and* how*?'*

Trust – Letting go doesn't have to mean that you lose control. You can define the outcomes that you want, and you can monitor progress. What you'll have to let go of is defining how things get done. You'll have to accept that different people will find different ways to reach the desired outcome that you set. We'll cover this in more detail when we look at Management and Metrics. Ask yourself, *'What are my main concerns with sharing control? What outcomes could I define without specifying how something should be done?'*

When is the right time?

The question of *when* to look for that business partner – the one who can complement your strengths and take on responsibilities that you not only don't enjoy but also aren't necessarily very good at – is a tricky one. For some businesses, focusing on hiring people to deliver products and services to their customers takes priority; for others, it's the technical team who builds their platform or supports their customers. My view is that once a team has grown beyond five or six people, most companies would benefit from shared leadership.

For Landbay, the decision to onboard a COO came at the end of their first year of trading. They viewed that first year as almost a 'proof of concept', showing the market and potential investors that their model could work, they'd built up the team and were ready to bring the tech in-house. John Goodall, Landbay's co-founder and CEO, told me that they needed to improve their governance and structure, especially as they were going through an authorisation process to become a regulated entity and had attracted significant external investment.

Pip Jamieson of The Dots knew that she needed a partner from the start. She told me about a 360 review that one of her mentors conducted when she exited her previous business. He talked to various people she had worked with, and looked for learnings she could take into her new business. The report identified her core strengths and recommended that she take on a CFO/COO so that she could focus on the product and building her business. She now mentors quite a few female founders who feel that they don't need a COO, but she told me that she's found employing one to be a critical factor in her ability to focus on developing the business.

Scott Erwin, CEO of Hire Hand, is a solo founder. He told me that he started off by chasing the problem, so that it was less about finding the team and more about finding the idea, really 'seeing' it. He told me that he had a moment where he thought, 'Oh gosh,

I've caught the problem, now I need help!' and that was when he started to build his team. He wanted to prove his hypothesis and get it robust enough to convince others before he looked for his team.

Many single founders discover that the moment they need a 'partner' is when they start fundraising. The time it takes to engage with investors and go through the whole process of raising funds is often underestimated. When I meet founders who are in that cycle, I ask them who's running their business. I usually get a quizzical look back, with the person wondering whether I was listening when they introduced themselves as managing director, CEO or founder. I ask them how connected to their business they're really able to feel as they spend days and days pitching, creating and reviewing documents and answering questions. Whether you choose to bring in a co-founder, COO or another senior role, it's wise to have someone keeping the plates spinning back in the business whilst you're out raising the funds you need to grow it.

Whatever the right time is for you, if you want to grow your business, you'll need to form partnerships with people who can help you scale – whether it be a formal partner or members of your team.

What kind of person?

It's important for you to understand your preferences. *Are you someone who prefers to inspire or to build? Do you get a buzz from thinking or doing? Are you better with people or with systems?* Naturally, business owners come in all shapes and sizes, and we're all wired differently, but in my experience, many entrepreneurs don't enjoy much of the actual running of their businesses and have no idea what needs to change. They feel that their choice is to either keep going as they are or to return to the world of employment. I'm here to offer you a third option, which is finding someone to run the business with you – someone who can figure out *how* while you focus on *what*.

Everyone has a creative side, and each one of us can get things done, but there's a magic that happens when an impatient, ambitious visionary meets a person who was born to implement. I was talking with Elroy 'Spoonface' Powell – musician, actor and entrepreneur – about how different people enjoy and are good at different activities. He looked at me incredulously and asked, 'You mean to say that there are people who actually enjoy data entry? I think something inside me has just exploded with joy!' Imagine if you could find a person who was good at and loved doing all the things in your business that you would rather not be doing.

When Elon Musk gave his frank interview to the *New York Times* (published 16 August 2018 - see Further Reading), one of the aspects that was largely overlooked by the media was the fact that Tesla had renewed its attempts to find a good COO to work alongside Musk and share the load. The company even approached Sheryl Sandberg to fill the role. She was brought in to Facebook in 2008, when the company was experiencing rapid growth and needed processes and systems to sustain its success. It was a similar story in March 2017 when Uber hit the headlines with embarrassing revelations about sexual harassment and regulatory avoidance and quickly announced that it was looking for a COO to work alongside CEO Travis Kalanick.

I find it surprising when companies of this size don't already have a COO. In my experience, every business needs one, even if it's small and the COO doesn't necessarily carry the title. What I also find interesting about these stories is that they demonstrate a real confusion about the COO's role, which varies widely from business to business. I think of a COO as the 'chief organising officer', the person who is running the company facing inwards, while the CEO faces outwards to customers, shareholders, investors and partners. The critical ingredient is the balance between the two individuals and the way their strengths, experience and preferences work together. Rather than getting too hung up on roles, start thinking about what kind of person could complement you and enhance your business.

Pip Jamieson of The Dots describes how COO and CFO John Down's attention to detail and focus on the finances allows her to lead the team and the vision and focus on product and business development.

John describes himself as a 'grenade jumper', which is a great description of a COO. He told me that he looks to take on anything that's going to suck up Pip's time. He recognises that the most precious commodity for most business owners, especially single founders, is time, and he sees his job as giving her back as much as possible. They both mention trust as a key element of what makes their partnership work.

Richard Royce, the COO of LawBite, told me, 'I've always enjoyed looking at the detail and the analysis and trying to work out why things are working and why they aren't, which has naturally led me into this field.' He told me that his experience in the music business – managing band members playing and touring together – was good practice for managing people in the business world, setting expectations and keeping the team happy.

Scott Erwin, CEO of Hire Hand, told me that he would look for someone who had had experience scaling up a business. 'I feel like I have a decent view of what happens once you get to fifty people, but from ten to fifty it's a real challenge. So I think learning from the wisdom of the other person is going to be a requirement for me.'

How to find the right person

Once they know what they're looking for, many entrepreneurs discover that they already have someone in their organisation who could step up into the role. Ask yourself, *'Who's the person who knows what's going on in my company (usually more than I do)? Who does my team turn to when I'm not there, when they don't want to bother me, or when they have some news that they think I won't like? Who's the person I turn to to talk things through with, who finds solutions to problems and makes sure that we keep on track?'* Whatever job title that person has in your company, they may have the ability to play a much more important role with the right support and guidance.

At a fundamental level, it's hard for many entrepreneurs to move from doing everything to sharing the load. This is the main reason why I tell people that the person they're looking for will probably come from their network.

Juliet Eccleston, co-founder and CEO of AnyGood?, told me about her thought process when approaching Carl Webber, her co-founder and COO. 'If this was going to work and we were going to do something with the business then it was going to be quite a big commitment and quite a bumpy ride. It can't just be based on somebody who's been a friend or somebody that you've kind of known in a work context for six months. It's got to be somebody where you've worked together on something that's been hard and you can trust completely. I can't imagine doing something like this with somebody I didn't know very well.'

John Goodall, co-founder and CEO of Landbay, told me that with his background in recruitment, he understood how challenging it can be to find good people, especially for key roles. He told me that 'having someone who you know and trust and respect' was an important part of his decision to appoint Julian Cork to the COO role. In fact, nearly all of the people I interviewed for this book chose to partner with someone they'd known or worked with before.

Pip Jamieson of The Dots worked with John Down at her previous company and knew that their skills were complementary. She told me, 'There is very little crossover in terms of our skill base.'

Clive Rich, founder, CEO and chairman of LawBite, had known Richard Royce for a number of years before approaching him to work together. Clive told me, 'I'm not one of those operators that likes to do everything themselves.' They worked together on a few different projects before LawBite took off.

Once you get clear about what you're looking for and what you can offer, it will be much easier to find the right person. You'll need a clear agreement on roles and responsibilities and a phased approach to bringing them in, but ultimately, growing a business requires you to trust other people. Trust is an important part of being a real entrepreneur.

Starting off right

When starting a business partnership, it's vital to have an open and honest conversation about what you want and why. Partnerships can break down for many reasons, but often they do so because expectations haven't been clearly stated from the start or because the partners realise that they don't want the same thing from the business. It's easy to muddle through when times are good, but when you hit a rough patch, being on the same page about what you're doing and why it's important can easily be the difference between staying together and drifting apart.

Partnership conversation tool

When advising entrepreneurs who are considering a business partnership (regardless of equity splits), I suggest a series of questions to get clear upfront:

- What are you trying to achieve with the business? What are your aspirations?

- Do you want to exit? If so, what's your time frame?

- What kind of business are you building – a lifestyle business to keep you and your family comfortable, or are you going for world domination?

- Who will be responsible for what? How is the effort to be split?

- What is the time commitment from each of the parties?

- What happens if one of you gets ill or dies?

- What happens if one of you falls pregnant or has a change in family circumstances?

- What happens if one of you changes their mind about time commitment or job role?

- What happens if one of you decides you want to leave earlier than planned?

- What happens if you don't agree?

Ultimately, a good partnership is founded on shared values, outcomes and timelines. People change and so do their priorities, expectations and goals, which is why it's so important to get clear upfront. It's much easier to have this conversation at the start, when things are harmonious and you're excited by the prospect of working together. After months or years of hard work, when things get tough and people discover that they want different things, or their memory of conversations becomes tainted by experience, the best of friends can end up falling out and never speaking to each other again. The passing of time and the stress of running a business can change your memory or perception of things. Even if you think you agree today, get it onto a piece of paper, just to be sure that you're (literally) on the same page. Something as simple as a memorandum of understanding can do wonders for clarifying what was agreed in a situation where both parties are convinced that their memory is correct.

John and Julian at Landbay don't have a formal split of responsibilities. They simply focus on what needs to be done. Juliet and Carl at AnyGood? found that their natural strengths pulled them into their distinct roles over time. Carl believes that going into a partnership with your eyes open is essential. 'Don't go into any kind of partnership thinking it's all going to be absolutely fine, it's an amazing idea and it's going to be so successful. Be prepared that it's not always going to be amazing and then look at the person that you're going to do it with and ask yourself if you believe it's going to work.' He explained that you have to ensure that you have the right level of trust and shared expectation to make the partnership work.

Clive of LawBite told me that the division of responsibilities between Richard and him happened quite organically. 'A lot of my focus is outwards, rather than inwards, whereas Richard has a fantastic capability to systemise, organise and present information. We didn't sit down on Day One and say right, I'm going to face outwards and you're going to face inwards, but I think that's how it works and I think it suits our temperaments. I think it's a good idea for a company if you can execute it [the partnership] properly.'

Making the partnership work

Finding the right person to work with can change your life. It will take work to make the partnership function smoothly, but the benefits are enormous.

- Shared workload – the most obvious benefit is that having someone else in at the 'top table' means less work for you

- Shared cognitive load – you have someone to share in decision-making and thinking things through

- Focus – having the right business partner will mean that you're able to focus on your strengths

- Backup – when you're having a bad day or things aren't going well, having someone there who has your back can be a welcome support

Pip Jamieson believes that the key elements that have made her partnership with John Down a success are their complementary skills and their ability to play to each other's strengths.

Clive Rich explained that running a high-growth company has its own set of challenges, not least the constant need for cash. For his COO, Richard, this has meant keeping the people and the technology in step with that growth trajectory. They experienced what every business founder or co-founder I've ever met has told me, which is that with five, six, even seven people you can keep in touch with everything that's happening, but as the team grows, structure must be introduced, which is what the Accountability pillar of the REAL model® is all about.

Being a real entrepreneur means recognising what your business needs, and there may come a time when that's no longer you. Playing to your strengths may mean bringing someone else in to run the business so you can focus on what you're good at (which might be starting the next one).

Partnership – Top three takeaways

1. An abundance mindset means being open to partnership

2. Find someone to complement your strengths, experience and preferences

3. Make sure expectations are clear from the start

CHAPTER FIVE

Team

'If you want to go fast, go alone. If you want to go far, go together.'

— African proverb

Many entrepreneurs will tell you that finding and keeping good people is one of the toughest parts of running a business. In fact, while many people get hung up on raising cash, it's actually a lack of talent that holds many businesses back. For businesses with variable demand and the need for a flexible workforce, the challenge can be a daunting one. The very nature of work is changing. As Scott Erwin from Hire Hand told me, 'Whether we want it to or not, the future of work will look more flexible and contingent. And actually, that's in keeping with many individuals' preferences, not just businesses trying to outsource.'

A lot has been written about millennials and how they want different things from the rest of us. In truth, every generation has developed its own way of doing things, but more and more people want flexibility in their working lives, whether they're twenty, forty or sixty. For many people, going into the same office every day and doing the same thing just isn't enough anymore, which presents some unique challenges for today's entrepreneur. Your team is the most important element of your small business 'jigsaw', but because so many people wait until they're swamped before they take on additional people, they often don't take the time to think about what kind of person the business actually needs. If your business is growing rapidly and you're desperate for help, you may be tempted to just hire anyone who seems reasonably competent, someone who can take some of the load off your shoulders. When you're panicking, just about anyone will do.

The problem is that if you're not sure what exactly you need, you're unlikely to get it. One bad hire can seriously derail you, especially in the early days. The cost of hiring the wrong person can be enormous for a small business, not just in terms of actual cash, but also in terms of the negative impact that the wrong hire can have on the team. At the other end of this process, it's hard to admit when you've made a mistake with your hiring. Ignore poor performance at your peril. Things are unlikely to improve without action being taken. Someone who isn't right for the team is probably draining you and your business, as well as demotivating and destabilising the team. If you keep panic hiring or not focusing on the team's overall makeup, the turnover of people in your business will increase, which will drain even more of your energy and time.

Because senior people are more expensive, it can be tempting to hire inexperienced juniors. What's often underestimated is the cognitive load on the entrepreneur. Rather than thinking about how to get it done, you often just want to know that it's being taken care of. If you're surrounded by junior people, you'll still be carrying a lot.

Organisations large and small spend a fortune on encouraging their people to improve on their weaknesses. How would it be if instead we asked our people to play to their strengths? Of course, it's possible to learn new skills and develop additional capabilities, but at our core, we are who we are. Why would you hire an accountant and get him working on his design skills? When people aren't playing to their strengths, it negatively affects their confidence and ability to feel that they're making progress. Trust and communication break down and motivation and engagement plummet. People may become disruptive and eventually leave if they're spending too much of their time doing things they don't enjoy or aren't well suited to.

Team – Play to peoples' strengths

Most successful people, whether they're entrepreneurs, sports stars or performers, talk about their team. They tell us that they couldn't have achieved what they did without the people around them. When British tennis player Andy Murray wins a match, he's quick to mention how his physio, coach and nutritionist played just as important a role as he did. Collaboration between individuals with complementary strengths, experience and preferences is a key element of building a successful business. Although we often hear that the customer is king, Richard Branson has a different perspective and is widely quoted as having said: 'Clients do not come first. Employees come first. If you take care of your employees, they will take care of the clients.' None of us have everything that is required to succeed. A real entrepreneur accepts this fundamental truth and looks for people who will complement them.

Some businesses have a clear structure in place when they set out, but many bring in the people they need as they grow. Juliet Eccleston, co-founder and CEO of AnyGood?, told me that she would look at what was taking up big chunks of their time, obvious areas of weakness or things that were requiring too much energy because they didn't have the knowledge and expertise between them, and then hire accordingly. Carl, her co-founder and COO, told me that trying to fill in a predetermined org chart would have taken a long time and would have been really frustrating, so instead they planned to find the right people and worked from there. In this chapter, we'll look at hiring and firing, how to find the right people and how to use psychometric profiling tools to build a great team.

Hiring and firing

Several of the people I interviewed acknowledged that for your first few team members, you're looking for a certain type of person. To quote Scott Erwin, the founder and CEO of Hire Hand, you need people with 'a certain level of risk threshold slash insanity to leave a stable job to join someone in a coffee shop with a laptop and an idea'. Which explains why early hires are often people who know and trust the founder. These early relationships can bring their own challenges as the business grows but are usually vital in getting the business off the ground.

It's easy to get dazzled by someone's credentials, but don't lose sight of the fact that you need to be able to work with them. If someone is going to make your whole team miserable, then it doesn't matter how great their experience or skills are – hiring them is always going to be the wrong thing to do.

Just as hiring too quickly can be a huge mistake, firing too slowly can have an equally devastating effect on your team. Most people dread having 'that' conversation, but often people know that something isn't right. If it's really not working, end it quickly and professionally. You may be surprised by how well the person takes the news. When you take the time to explain in clear, rational terms why it's not working, you'll often get a reasonable response – the person may even be relieved. Julian at Landbay told me that when they've had to let people go, in most cases, it's been an easier conversation than expected with the person recognising that the feedback is fair and agreeing that it isn't really working out. John and Pip at The Dots told me that all their senior team are 'try before you buy'. In other words, they started out as contractors before becoming employees.

Finding the right people

Whether you're looking for a new full-time member of the team, an outsourced specialist or a part-time person to fill a gap, recruitment can be a time-consuming and draining process for you and your business. Here's a handy tool to run through next time you're looking to add to your team or change the way you're structured.

People finder tool

1. **Be clear about why you're hiring.** It's important to consider options, including outsourcing, restructuring or automation, to ensure that you get what you need. Make sure you've considered whether members of your current team might be able to fill the gap and give them the opportunity to pitch for the role if they're interested. Ask

yourself, *'Why am I hiring? Do I need a person or a service?'*

2. **Be clear about what you need.** Make sure you know what the gap is in your organisation and what you feel is missing. A key decision will be whether to engage a junior or a senior person. It will likely come down to whether you want someone you can mould or someone who can come in and take ownership. This is about attitude as much as it's about experience. In general, junior people are cheaper and easier to control, but they'll need more direction than a good senior person. Junior people can be trained to take on more responsibility and ownership over time, whereas senior people may come in with their own ideas (usually welcome, but can be challenging to manage). A good compromise may be to find a hands-on senior person who will figure out what needs to be done, start off doing it themselves and then build a team under them as your company grows. I would encourage you to get clear about what kind of person you need before you start the process. If you don't, then you risk retrofitting your decision around someone you like, rather than someone who's the right fit for your organisation. Ask yourself, *'What kind of person am I looking for?'*

3. **Be clear about the role.** Think through whether you need them full-time or part-time, on a contract or permanent basis. Location, start date

and length of engagement are other important factors to consider. The skills and experience you're looking for will depend on how you see the person fitting into your existing team. Someone who's good at setting up or building a system, process or team may not be the person who'll be best at running or managing it, so bear that in mind during this process. A good job description or role profile is an essential part of setting clear expectations upfront.

Many people will look for industry or sector knowledge and may place a premium on certain skills or knowledge. These things can be taught over time, whereas attitude and instinct cannot. I recommend ensuring that you have a balance of focus through your interviewing process. If you tend to prioritise knowledge, make sure that you have someone in the process who's assessing attitude and instinct. I like to ask people I'm interviewing what makes them get out of bed in the morning (apart from having to pay the bills) and what makes them have a good or bad day.

Don't forget that while people tend to hire for skill, they usually fire for behaviour, so include questions aimed at assessing how people conduct themselves. Ask for examples of how they've dealt with particular situations rather than imagining what they might do, so that you can get a sense of their thought processes, instincts and experience. Try to understand what makes them tick and why they believe in your business and want to be a part of it. All team members contribute to your company's culture, but especially the early hires. Focus on getting people with the right attitude and values into the team and they'll help you build the kind of business you want. Your organisation is the sum of its people and therefore will change and grow and learn as they do. Ask yourself, *'What is the role? How do I describe it clearly? What do I need to understand about the person I am looking for?'*

4. **Be clear about who will be involved in the recruitment process.** Empower your management team, if you have one, and give them the responsibility for making decisions. Depending on who you're hiring, you may want to be part of the process, but there's no need for you to manage the whole thing.

To execute this process quickly and efficiently, run a mini assessment centre. Bring in several candidates for a couple of hours, brief them on the company and the role and then rotate them round several members of your team, who will interview each for twenty minutes focusing on different areas you want covered. You might have one person looking at skills, another at experience. You might also focus on behaviours and how well someone will fit into the existing team. At the end of this process, each team member gives their score for each candidate and an offer can be put together immediately. This approach prevents anyone in your team from being influenced by other opinions as all scores are submitted at the same time. Ask yourself, *'Who can help me find the right person?'*

5. **Be clear about your expectations.** The final piece is helping the person integrate into the team. One of the biggest sources of anger, disquiet and anxiety is unmet expectations, so make sure you give each member of your team plenty of guidance on what you need and feedback on how they're performing. Be clear about the standards required and any improvements to be made. As you'd do with anybody else in your team, focus on what you want done rather than how you'd do it. We all do things differently, and it can be incredibly frustrating having a control-freak boss looking over your shoulder and telling you how to do things. Empower your people to do their jobs and accept that mistakes will happen. Ask yourself, *'What are my expectations of this role?'*

Many small businesses don't bother with role profiles or job descriptions on the basis that everyone is mucking in together and doing what needs to be done. To a certain extent this is true, especially in the early days, but the need for clarity is likely to come sooner than you think. Without clear role profiles, tasks will start to get missed and fall between the cracks, and people may overlap and work on the same thing without realising it. This 'blurring' can quickly lead to misunderstandings, differences in expectations and conflict. A simple role profile detailing clear roles and responsibilities can cure a lot of problems.

I did some work with a client who had six different levels of seniority within his small business, which is typical of the industry he operates in. Talking to members of the team, I found a lot of confusion, misunderstanding and resentment around promotions and pay scales. It was unclear to them what exactly the levels were and the criteria to achieve each one. The management team worked on a clear role profile for each level, showing the progression on each aspect of each role, and then shared it with the wider team. Now everyone can clearly see not just what their own responsibilities are but also those of their teammates. They can have sensible conversations with their managers about where they are today and where they want to get to, rather than feeling like job titles and promotions are managed in a vacuum at the whim of the owner.

Psychometric profiling tools

Enabling your people to deploy their energies and natural talents to run your business and serve your customers is a good way to get positive energy flowing through your business. You need to have a good understanding of who's in your team today, what strengths you need to complement what you have and how to fit them together into a productive unit. As Stephen Covey is quoted as saying, 'Strength lies in differences, not in similarities.'

Psychometric (from the Greek words for 'mental' and 'measurement') profiling tools can be a good way to help your team understand themselves and each other in an objective way using a common language. These tools typically measure interests, personality and aptitude and can increase productivity, communication and trust. They're often used during the recruitment process to remove bias and assess a candidate's values, motivating factors and aptitude in areas such as decision-making and teamwork.

There are many profiling tools to choose from (I've included a comparison of five different tools in the Further Reading section). I use Talent Dynamics because it's based on the Chinese concept of *qi*, which loosely translates to 'life force', 'flow' or 'energy'. This link to energies and flow resonates strongly with me as well as with many of my clients and people I speak with. Roger Hamilton, the creator of Wealth Dynamics and Talent Dynamics, in an article published on GeniusU.com on 30 June, 2013 (see Further Reading), describes flow as 'your path of least resistance', which I find most people can immediately relate to. I've also heard it described as the state between being bored and being stressed – when you're in the 'zone'.

Profiling tools can be used in one-to-one meetings, small focused sessions or team workshops to increase understanding and productivity. I find Talent Dynamics a really useful tool to start a conversation about how different we all are. This can help take the personal 'sting' out of situations. Instead of thinking that someone is being deliberately annoying by asking for more time and more data before making a decision, we can understand that this is their natural preference and they're not purposefully trying to slow things down. When we feel that someone is moving too fast or making decisions too quickly, we can choose not to take it personally but instead explain that although their preference is to move fast, and act on instinct, others need more information before being able to take the next step. When we think that someone is being cold and uncaring, or, at the opposite extreme, making friends with everyone they meet, we can understand that we're all wired differently and some need more interaction with people than others.

Our natural preferences mean that some activities will take more or less energy from us. For example, someone who prefers lots of detail and research could learn how to be a great public speaker. They could become very skilled at it and receive lots of compliments, and no one would ever guess that it wasn't in their flow. But however many times they got up on their feet and spoke, it would still take a lot of their energy and they would still end the day feeling drained. Those of us who aren't particularly great with details could spend a few hours with a spreadsheet and might do a great job, but we would probably feel pretty exhausted afterwards.

We all have a certain amount of energy every day, and it's up to us how we choose to use it. There are no right or wrong profiles. You can choose to do a job amazingly well and still be out of flow. It will take up much more of your energy than one where you spend more time in flow, but that in no way means that you can't be good at it if you wish. As a real entrepreneur, how much of your time do you spend in flow? If you could find a way to increase that, what would it do for your productivity and for your energy levels?

It's important to emphasise that these tools aren't designed to test a person's capabilities but instead to look at their natural preferences. Whenever I run a team workshop, someone usually asks if something is wrong with them, or worries that the tool will be used to judge their performance or capability. I always tell them that our profile is not a predictor of our likely career path, not the only solution to a problem and definitely not an excuse to behave badly. It's a tool to find our flow, a way for others to see our value and leverage it.

It can be a powerful experience to get a group of colleagues together, looking at how they're all wired and discussing how that impacts communication, productivity and ultimately trust. People quickly learn the difference between extroverts and introverts (where you get your energy from rather than how loud and confident you are!) and this can lead to really life-changing conversations. A man came up to me after one such session. 'That was energising,' he told me. 'I feel like it's OK to be me. I've learned more about myself today than I have in the past ten years!' The truth is that many introverts feel undervalued and unappreciated in a world where the people who shout loudest usually get the most attention. Susan Cain, author of *Quiet: The Power of Introverts in a World That Can't Stop Talking* (Penguin, 2012), makes the point clearly and simply, 'There's zero correlation between being the best talker and having the best ideas.' The truth is that you need a mix of energies and profiles in order to grow a successful business and once everyone in your team understands their value, the increase in motivation, commitment and happiness can be profound.

Here are my top tips for using psychometric tests in your business.

Using psychometric tests

1. Profile your whole team.

2. Use the profiles in discussions with key individuals to help them understand each other and work together better – sometimes this may lead to people wanting to shift roles or take on

more or different responsibilities, so be ready to have this conversation.

3. Run workshops – get a specialist in to run a session for your team or each of your teams (depending on the size of your business) focused on communication, productivity and trust. Understanding is a good start, but the benefits come from the actions that you take as a team as a result of this new knowledge.

4. Use the profiles to build or strengthen your management team – pick people who will complement you and help you drive the business forward.

5. Consider developing an energy chart to sit alongside your organisational chart – an insightful way to look at your team.

6. Use profiling during your recruitment process to ensure that you have a good fit of not just skills and experiences but also preferences.

As a real entrepreneur, your job is to provide your team with clarity and consistency. When people know where they are, they have clarity, even if they don't like it. Lack of clarity causes tension and stress. When we don't understand why things work the way they do, we tend to stick our heels in and resist. It's important to recognise that not everyone will be able to come with you on the journey. Growing a business is a rollercoaster that doesn't suit everyone. As Scott

Erwin told me, people who are the perfect fit for the first or second year might not be able to adapt as your business evolves. 'The key is to continue to articulate the vision and just trust that [you'll] be able to attract the right people at the right stage.'

Team – Top three takeaways

1. Have a clear recruitment process that involves members of your team

2. Setting clear expectations reduces anger, disquiet and anxiety

3. Understanding the people around you is key to building a strong and productive team

CHAPTER SIX

Customer

'Don't find customers for your products, find products for your customers.'

— Seth Godin, American author and entrepreneur

When we start a new business, our first challenge is to find one customer. One person or organisation who has a problem, who can see the value of our product or service in fixing that problem, and who is prepared to trust us and pay us money. Our focus needs to be on giving that one customer our absolute best, with total commitment to solving their problem. Until we know that the value we're providing is real – in our customer's eyes – there's no point in spending lots of money or time on branding, websites and fancy brochures. Roger Hamilton is quoted as saying, 'A business isn't a business because it has a product, a business is a business when it has a customer', and a real entrepreneur never loses sight of their customer.

As we take on more and more customers, it can be all too easy to become disconnected from them. Too many business owners are so focused on finding new customers that they forget the ones they already have. When we get too busy and overwhelmed, our tendency is to withdraw and focus on the day-to-day of the business. We can get distracted and frustrated putting in complicated systems and taking on too many people. But staying connected to customers is a vital part of an entrepreneur's life. You need to be soliciting feedback, using trial and error and constantly questioning the value of what your business is delivering to its customers.

In years gone by, the challenge for an entrepreneur was to be the best in their local area. Competition was known and usually local. Today, your customers may be accessing products and services from the other side of the world. Your competition is everywhere, but so are your potential customers. With so much choice available, there's constant pressure on prices, and many businesses struggle to survive.

If you're finding it hard to increase the number of customers who will do business with you, you need to take a look at your value proposition and the service you're providing. Are you really offering something that people want as well as need?

Customer – Deliver value

Your customers are the only people who can really help you figure out the value of what you're selling. Your job is to resolve their critical problems with solutions that deliver real value. To avoid creating a load of products and services that no one wants, spend as much time as you can with your customers to understand what they need and what they want. When you start out, and you're in the process of understanding these needs and wants, this is absolutely critical. Scott Erwin of Hire Hand explained it perfectly when he told me that tech start-ups in particular shouldn't be 'having an idea and having the market come to [them], but rather seeing where the market is and trying to go to it'. The implications of this are that your business may look radically different at ten months than it does at two. In this chapter, we'll look at identifying your customers, attracting your customers, your value proposition, how to rate your customers and how to ensure that the lines of communication stay open.

Identifying your customers

You can't be all things to all people. You can't improve everyone's life. The best performing companies make a clear decision to understand who their target customers are – what their big problems are, what matters most to them, what they want most and what they value. Your solution must genuinely improve the lives of your target customers.

People generally don't want to choose a niche because they fear not attracting enough clients or enough money, or they fear getting bored and feeling stuck. Even though all the evidence points to people doing much better when they focus on a niche (see the links in Further Reading), people still fear 'turning away' business. The truth is that you're not turning anyone away – you're actively targeting a specific set of people with a particular problem that you can solve. Once you own your niche and are seen as an expert to those customers, you can always expand into other niches. The best way to learn what your customers want is to really get to know them and how to provide value to them. You can only do that if you know who they are.

The hardest thing for so many business owners is to choose a niche. One of my favourite ways of describing this process to my customers is to tell them that they must stand in a room of 1,000 doors and pick one. Put another way, if you can't summarise your business in one sentence, then you don't truly know your own business.

However long you've been in business and however clear you believe you are, this tool is worth revisiting at least annually. Although we think of customers as a group, each customer is an individual making individual decisions and thinking only of themselves. Even if you sell into large businesses that have complicated approval processes and multi-layered decision-making, each of the people involved is an individual with their own opinions and motivations. The more detail you can get into, the more targeted and impactful your communication and interactions will be.

Who is my customer tool

Develop a persona of your ideal client – who they are, how they live and what they do.

1. **Demographics**
   Age, male/female, nationality, sexuality, education, job, size of company they work in, how much money they have/earn, relationship status, children, living arrangements, what kind of house/car they have, where they live/work, where they shop/socialise/exercise, how they get to work, how far they live from work

2. **Lifestyle**
   Hobbies, feelings about job/family/life, worries/ stresses/delights, voting preferences and patterns, what they care about, why they do what they do, why they live where they live, what they are proud/ashamed of, why they would want to work with you

3. **Interests**

   What type of books, newspapers, magazines, music, videos, podcasts, channels they read / watch / listen to, where they get their information, who they talk to / trust, what professional content they consume, which websites they visit, what groups / associations they belong to, how they spend their money and on what

If you are struggling with this, think about these questions:

- Who can you help the most?

- Who can afford to pay?

- Who do you like / want to work with?

Imagine that these questions are three circles that partially overlap – your customer sits in the centre where all three circles meet.

Attracting your customers

Now think about your customer's problems, what mistakes they're making and what they really want. You're really trying to get inside their heads, creating a psychographic profile if you will.

1. **Problems**

   What stresses them out? What do they worry about? What do they want more or less of? What would they fix if money or time wasn't an issue?

2. **Mistakes**

   What are they thinking wrong and doing wrong and why is this a problem for them? It's important to get clear on this to build trust with your potential customers.

3. **What they really want**

   Often, there's a question that your ideal customer is asking, and if this question was answered, most of their problems would disappear. Everybody is chasing feelings, so how do you want your customer to feel? We all buy on emotion and then rationalise using logic. We buy what we want rather than what we need. The job of a real entrepreneur is to find a way to give our customers what they want as well as what they need.

Being totally clear on how you improve people's lives shapes the way you recruit, unite, move, touch and inspire everyone who connects with your business, from employees and suppliers right through to end customers (who ultimately vote with their wallets and feet).

Your value proposition

It's important to be clear about your service strategy. What will your service look like? What kind of experience do you want to give your customers? Are you aiming for great service (which comes at a cost) or adequate service (because you want to keep costs low)? It's not possible to offer both, and this decision is one that's important to consider carefully. In *The Effortless Experience: Conquering the New Battleground for Customer Loyalty* (Penguin, 2013), authors Matthew Dixon, Nick Toman and Rick DeLisi argue that trying to delight your customers is costly and overrated, and that loyalty is what really counts. Loyalty comes from solving your customers' problems and being easy to do business with. Your value proposition must include making sure your customers know that you care. As Theodore Roosevelt famously said, 'Nobody cares how much you know until they know how much you care.' You might be the best at what you do, but customers want to feel that they're important to you.

Not all customers are created equal

It's really important to have in your mind who your ideal customer is and why. If you think of your customers in terms of the time and effort involved in serving them and the profit you make on them, an interesting picture starts to emerge. Your A-grade customers are those who take low effort and make you high profit. Those who take high effort but make you high profit are also worth keeping. But as your business becomes more established, you may find that you continue to serve some customers who make you low profit. I often find that business owners 'hang on' to early customers out of a sense of loyalty or emotion, just as they may do with early stage employees. This isn't necessarily the right thing either for your business or for your customers. If they're also not taking much effort, you might be able to increase their profitability by offering them different services or flexing the support you give them, but those that make you a low profit and take a lot of effort to serve are the ones you really want to take a close look at.

The interesting thing is that your D-grade customers may represent somebody else's A- or B-grade customers. You may be able to do a deal with someone who wants to scale up in a different way than you, perhaps by focusing on volume rather than value – your customers might be perfect for them. It's worth reviewing your list of customers once a year and ensuring that you're maximising your resources and also serving your customers in the best way. Sometimes a move may be the right thing for all parties.

Communicating with customers

As we introduce technology and processes to help us grow our business, it's easy to become disconnected from our customers. Some businesses forget how important it is to stay in regular contact with their customers to ensure they're continuing to deliver value to them.

Here are some handy tips on how to keep the lines of communication open with your customers.

Staying in touch

1. **The Pareto principle** – Also known as the 80/20 rule, this principle states that roughly 80% of the effects come from 20% of the causes. This means that 80% of your sales are likely to come from 20% of your customers (more information can be found in the Further Reading section). Your primary focus shouldn't be on finding new customers but on making sure your existing customers are happy, buying more from you and telling their friends! Ask yourself, *'What are we doing for our existing customers?'*

2. **Going the extra mile** – Trust is critical in all relationships, including those with our customers. Like us, they do business with people they trust, those who take the time to get to know and understand them, listen to their problems and go the extra mile to help solve them. Make sure that you're rewarding team members who do that little bit extra for their customers. Ask yourself, *'How are we going the extra mile? How am I rewarding those in the team that do?'*

3. **Personal touches** – If you're selling to other businesses, it can be easy to forget that you're still dealing with individual people. An organisation doesn't make a decision or feel a certain way – people do. And most people appreciate the personal touch and attempts to build rapport – a follow-up call or message or a genuine enquiry about how they're doing will not go unnoticed. When people are making their next buying decisions, these little touches can make all the difference. Ask yourself, *'What personal touches do we have in our sales and marketing processes?'*

4. **Communication.** To cut through the mountain of information that most people are confronted with every day, ensure that you're using different channels to get your message out – whether it's social media, blogging, articles, videos or emails (to name but a few options). Your customers will need a reason to contact you, so make sure you're keeping them informed of what's new and relevant to them. Ask for their opinion and take any opportunity to interact as long as it's valuable for your customer. Ask yourself, *'How are we communicating with our customers? What reasons do they have to talk to us?'*

5. **Mistakes are good.** If handled right, customer complaints can actually be a positive thing. Showing them how much you care about resolving their issues can often transform an unhappy customer into one who is even more

loyal and satisfied than they were before the issue occurred. Ask yourself, *'What are we doing to fix mistakes? How do we show our customers that we care?'*

Remember that however much you niche, your customers are all different. Many hairdressers hire bubbly, chatty people on the assumption that everyone wants a good old natter while having their hair cut. But by doing this, how many of their customers are gritting their teeth and 'being polite' and how many potential great hairdressers are you turning away because you and they both think that being very chatty is important to all customers? If you focus on the value that you're delivering to each and every one of your customers, you won't go far wrong. As Ken Blanchard, author of *Leading at a Higher Level: Blanchard on How to be a High Performing Leader* (Financial Times/Prentice Hall, 2010), said, 'Profit is the applause you get for taking care of your customers and creating a motivating environment for your people.'

Customer – Top three takeaways

1. Understanding your customer is key to the success of your business

2. Choosing a niche to own will enable you to reach and serve your target customers

3. Establish and maintain lines of communication with your customers

Bringing Energy together

Energy isn't something you have but something you create. It's about playing to your strengths and using the power of the team – different people, from different backgrounds and with different experiences, coming together to deliver value to your customers. Understanding how you're wired and what your preferences are is absolutely critical. Trying to do everything yourself is a sure way to feel overwhelmed, defeated and guilty. Consider what kind of person might complement you in terms of strengths and see how it feels to spend some time together talking about your business. If they're the right person, you'll probably find that they have a very different approach and perspective than you. As Marc Benioff, co-CEO of Salesforce, is quoted as saying, 'The secret to successful hiring is this: look for people who want to change the world.' Get good people in, give them the tools they need to do their jobs and then get out of their way so that they can serve your customers. To be a real entrepreneur, you need to see your business as separate from you – something that's more than the sum of its parts; something to be nourished and cared for.

- What are your key takeaways from the Energy section?

- What are you going to implement immediately?

- What are you looking at differently now?

PART THREE

A IS FOR ACCOUNTABILITY

Many entrepreneurs dream of finding people to take ownership within their businesses. 'If only my people would step up' is a common complaint. Accountability is at the core of every successful business. It cannot be given, only taken. It's about ownership and feeling responsibility for actions, decisions and outcomes. Without people who feel accountable, you'll find it tough to grow your business. Sharing the load and playing to people's strengths leads to the need for structure as you scale, so that each person understands the value that they bring to the team. Delivering consistent, high-quality service to each and every customer is a cornerstone of the REAL model®, bringing much-needed structure to your growing business.

If your team is unclear about who is working on what, if there are overlapping roles and responsibilities or if delivery to your customers is inconsistent, then this section is where to start. If you're feeling that you're spread 'too thin', finding it difficult to trust your people or realising that all roads in your business still lead back to you, then this section will give you ways of looking at what you do from a different perspective, allowing you to learn how to let go. If decision-making is unclear in your business, your team is likely to be feeling demotivated. Your business may seem out of control with unpleasant surprises being more common than you'd like. This section will help you bring in the structure that your business needs to thrive.

Accountability starts with everyone in the team knowing what each person is responsible for and understanding each interaction that your customer has with you and how you want them to feel at each stage. It means collective responsibility and decision-making and measuring the key things in your business to stay on track.

CHAPTER SEVEN

Operations

'Systems run the business and people run the systems.'
— Michael Gerber, author of *The E-Myth*

Not every business has the potential to impact the lives of its customers in the way that an airline can, if it fails to implement its maintenance procedures. When military procedures break down, 'friendly fire' incidents happen. When banking software isn't properly managed, systems fail and people cannot access their money; when regulations fail or are absent, a worldwide financial collapse is possible.

Building up a business is an evolutionary process. You may have started off with a few part-timers, grabbing favours from people whenever and wherever you could. You did what it took to get the job done, to build your product and to service your first customers. Typically, teams learn as they grow, with different people bringing their own skills and experiences to the mix. Different ways of doing things often emerge, and as your business grows and takes on more people, it's not uncommon to have various parts of an organisation doing the same thing in different ways.

Many small businesses don't have an organisation chart, but if they were to draw one, it might look a bit like a plate of spaghetti, with overlapping lines and connections and maybe the odd blob of sauce where nobody quite knows what's happening. This is normal in small businesses, but it can lead to confusion and conflict, overlapping responsibilities and things falling through the cracks.

When you're constantly firefighting, it's almost impossible to see your business with the clarity that's required. You may not even realise how much inconsistency has crept in. You may be too close to the people, too involved in the day-to-day or unable to keep all the balls in the air. It's relatively easy to muddle through without systems and processes when you're starting out and have a small team, but as your business grows and you bring more people in, the knowledge contained within your business will get diluted.

Your customers may never quite know what level of service they're going to get. One day your team might deliver a top-quality experience, and the next day they might miss things or repeat each other. If your customers don't know what to expect from you, they're much less likely to continue to do business with you.

This is likely to be hugely frustrating for your people who want to do a good job. They're often the ones who bear the brunt of your customers' dissatisfaction and who feel the impact of chaos and confusion. If your people don't know what's expected of them, quality and communication will become inconsistent, and ultimately, trust with your customers, suppliers and team will break down.

When people leave or are away from your business on holiday or off sick, there may be tasks that get left undone, promises to customers or suppliers that slip or important dates that get missed. This can lead to lost orders, dissatisfied customers and money being left on the table. When new people join the team, it takes time to bring them up to speed so that they understand what's expected of them and how what they do fits into the overall process of serving your customers and running your business.

For some people, the word 'process' or 'system' has negative connotations, such as constriction and slowness, conformity and lack of innovation, poor flexibility and inhibited creativity. For others, processes and systems represents freedom, rigour, security and the comfort and confidence of knowing what's happening. For your customers, it's the way you deliver a consistent, high-quality service to them every single time. It's the way to become easy to deal with.

Operations – Be easy to deal with

For every business, there comes a time to think about structure. For some businesses it will come earlier than for others, depending on your business model and what you're selling, but to scale, you'll need to address it at some point.

For Landbay, the time came when they secured institutional investment. Their focus shifted from raising retail finance to executing loans quickly and efficiently. Julian Cork, Landbay's COO, told me that they did a lot of work to 'industrialise' their processes. They have a clear idea of what kind of business they're building and are focused on the 'target state' of each process – ie what they want it to look like in the future. He said, '[We want] a structure that thinks about being a 100-person organisation when we're a thirty-person organisation becoming a fifty-person organisation. It's just what we do and how we do things.'

Whyte & Co had to adapt to changes in legislation when the poll tax was introduced in the UK. Their business had been centred around self-employed bailiffs who spent all their time out on the road, but the changes in legislation meant that they also needed to have an office, employ a team and be able to receive payments on behalf of local councils. Administratively, it was hugely manual – recording payments in ledgers and lots of paper filing. Over the years, most of their manual systems have been replaced by technology which has fully automated the recovery cycle, bringing cost savings and improved efficiencies in performance to clients.

Clive Rich of LawBite told me, 'As any company grows, you need processes in order to be scalable. We've put a lot of processes in place and been systematic about it. It is really key, I think, to be truly scalable.' He said that designing processes in advance of the problem (hitting the point where you need to systemise) is quite challenging. 'Strategy is important at the beginning to ensure you set off in the right direction, and then when you reach a certain size clearly it makes a big difference, but right in that middle bit, when you're climbing out of the swamp, it just doesn't feel that important. When you're growing there are overriding operational imperatives, principally revenue, that sort of barge everything else out of the way. It's all about each day, each week, each month. Which doesn't leave a lot of time for thinking, planning or process mapping!'

The speed or urgency with which you need to focus on your business model and its operations may also be governed by whether you're a high- or low-volume business. Scott Erwin of Hire Hand explained that in a low-margin, high-volume business like his, you have no choice but to be thinking about efficiency, automation and systemisation right from the start. He told me that he didn't have the 'luxury of just winging it', otherwise he would have burned through his resources in an unsustainable way. Instead, he put considerable effort into thinking about the right business model for Hire Hand upfront and tested it thoroughly before growing his team and seeking investment. He consciously wanted to avoid being one of those companies that scale up with huge fanfare and then suddenly find themselves abandoned by investors who realise that the company will never be profitable with their chosen business model. In this chapter, we'll look at processes and systems, the journey you want your customer to take through your business and how to build the delivery engine of your business.

Processes and systems

The words 'process' and 'system' are often used interchangeably, but it can be helpful to think about the difference.

A **process** is a sequence of events that enables things to get done. You start with an input, you have a few steps and you end with an output. If a potential customer calls you up, what happens next? Who does what? A **system** is the tool or method that's used to execute the process – how you get the job done.

Generally, processes address effectiveness or doing the right things, whereas systems address efficiency or doing things right. If you're doing the right things too slowly or inconsistently, look at improving your systems – is there a piece of technology that could help you or a different way of doing things? If you're working fast but not really getting anywhere, look at how your processes could be improved. Do you have too many different people involved? Is there a way of simplifying what you do? Always focus on processes if you're not sure.

In an ideal world, systems support processes which support people. For example, the Dropbox system makes the process of sharing and collaborating on files easier for people, and allows them to avoid emailing potentially sensitive documents, creating multiple copies or losing a vital piece of information.

Here's what your systems and processes should be doing for you.

Process and system checklist

1. **Setting expectations with your customers.** Even though you want your customers to feel special and you may want to offer them a personalised service, behind the scenes, you need predictable processes and systems to deliver the same high value to everyone in a consistent way. Many small businesses get caught in the trap of offering

bespoke products or services to each customer, which is extremely difficult to scale. This is why many companies offer Gold, Silver and Bronze packages. They may give customers the ability to tweak their package, but internally most of what's happening is predictable and repeatable. This gives customers confidence and certainty.

2. **Supporting your team.** Well-designed processes and systems are easy to learn and replicate, and they leave your team free to delight their customers. As you take on more people, they can integrate and learn much easier and quicker with good processes and systems. These processes and systems can be designed to be flexible to allow your team to share responsibility, support each other and feel empowered. When everyone understands their role in the overall process of delivering a high-quality experience to every customer, trust between teammates increases. Once everyone knows their role and what's expected of them, you can relax and resist any urge you may have to look over your shoulder.

3. **Saving you money.** A good delivery process will avoid repetition and rework and help keep costs down. Quality assurance leads to consistency of output and prevents extra work. Having good processes and systems in place will also ensure that you make best use of your resources and don't miss any opportunities to offer your customers even more value.

4. **Setting you free.** If you want to get out of the day-to-day running of your business so that you can focus on driving it forward, you'll need robust processes and systems. Processes need to be designed to involve you only at very specific points. Avoid becoming the bottleneck in a process. Instead, be the person that your team comes to when the process breaks down and they are unable to fix it, or when they need a decision they don't feel that they can make. Empower your team to run things without you and add value where you're actually needed.

Getting good processes in place and documented can be time-consuming, but it's not something that you need to be doing yourself. As a real entrepreneur, you want to be empowering your teams to document what they do, share this information with others, including you, and then take onboard everyone's feedback and insights. These documents are critical assets for a growing business and need to be kept up-to-date, refined and revisited regularly, especially when mistakes are made. You're building the engine of your business and want it to run as efficiently and strongly as possible.

Customer journey

So where and how to start? Which process should you begin with? In her book *Process to Profit – Systemise your Business to Build a High Performing Team and Gain*

More Time, More Control and More Profit (Rethink Press, 2013), Marianne Page recommends thinking about your business as if you want to set up a franchise model, even if this isn't the way you want to take your business. Considering what you would need to do to replicate your business in a different location or industry is a great way to get yourself thinking about systems and processes.

My advice is to get your team started with the core processes of your business – how you find customers and how you deliver your product or service to them. The core process of most businesses is referred to as the 'Customer Journey'. Here's how to map it out.

Customer journey tool

1. **High-Level Steps.** Think about what you do with and for your customers in five high-level steps. First, you identify them; second, you attract them; third, you convert them; fourth, you deliver value; and fifth, you reflect and improve.

2. **Grid.** Create a simple grid with multiple rows and four columns – Step, Description, Feeling and Assessment.

3. **Detailed Steps.** Break down each of the five high-level steps into more detail. List each of the steps your customer takes in the first column. Think about what's happening from the moment they start looking (even if they don't know exactly

what they want/need yet) to the time your service is finished and you want to keep the relationship and conversation going. Make sure you include how you communicate with customers and how they give you feedback.

4. **Description.** In the second column, describe what's going on during each step. Who's doing what? How long does it take? What's the desired outcome?

5. **Feeling.** Think about how you want your customer to feel during each step – supported, surprised, delighted? Add this to the third column of your grid.

6. **Assessment.** As a team, score how you think your business is doing today (out of ten). How easy are you to do business with? What could be done to improve this score? Add this to the final column of the grid.

Once the grid is complete, the team can present it to their colleagues and ask them for constructive feedback. Encourage challenge and debate across teams. Look at where the blockers are and how long each step takes. This can be a hugely powerful exercise, especially as your business grows and takes on more people. Our tendency is to focus on 'our bit', which can cause confusion and mistrust between teams. Cross-training and knowledge-sharing is essential as well, and ensuring that everyone in your business feels responsible for consistency and continuity.

I first learned this tool when I was training to be a project manager in a large corporate. I still remember the powerful impact of getting a group of people together from different parts of a process and mapping it out step by step. The conversations and insights that people got from understanding *what* other people do and *why* have stayed with me over the years. This tool can be used in whatever industry or sector you're in, and whatever size of business. Here's a practical example from a company with a team of sixteen.

An architect client of mine noticed significant inconsistencies regarding how his various project managers were running their projects. I suggested that we get them to work together to agree on the 'company way' of delivering projects to customers.

The project managers and I started with a discussion about what the purpose of this work was and what the output would be used for. They agreed that it would be useful to have one way of doing things that could be shared with the whole team so that everyone was on the same page. For more junior team members who work on multiple projects, it would mean having a common framework from which to work. The next step was to agree what the high-level phases of a project should be and where each phase should start and end. The insights they all gained from that discussion were really interesting. They'd never had any reason to wonder how their fellow project managers were structuring their projects, and it came as quite a surprise to them how much variation there was between each of them.

Once we'd agreed on the phases, we discussed what information they wanted to capture about each phase (what's required to start and exit each phase and what needs to be delivered), and the team then broke off into smaller groups. They took responsibility for the different phases, all working to a common format. Next, we had a series of sessions where we looked at each phase in detail, with the team who'd worked on it presenting their logic and explanations to the other project managers.

We had agreed upfront that we wouldn't present the finished process to the senior managers of the business until all the project managers were in agreement. The process of working together over a number of weeks meant that people who didn't normally work together were collaborating, and they all got important insights and perspectives about their role from others doing the same job but in different ways.

The next steps were to present their work to the management team, gather their feedback and then share the final document with the whole team. Even at this point there was more consistency between the project managers. The final step was for this shared view of how to do things to be taken forward and embedded in company procedure so that it became 'the way we do things here'.

How to build your delivery engine

In the Partnership chapter, we spoke about the importance of working with someone with strengths that complement your own. While one of you focuses on marketing and selling, building the brand, attracting attention and spreading the word, the other can be building the engine of the business that will deliver on all those promises.

I advise the person who is 'building' to invest the time and effort as early as possible. Every time you introduce something new, think about how it could be systemised and repeated. Every time you make a mistake, learn from it and put in place a simple process or mechanism to ensure that the organisation learns. The first time you bill a customer, draw up a contract or deliver a product, there's so much learning involved. Every time a problem crops up – maybe you got the payment terms wrong and you struggle with cash flow – fix it but also think about how to avoid it in the future. Do you need to create a template? Add it to your list of documents that get reviewed regularly. Does your team need training or information? Try to think about your business as a much larger entity from the very start. This will enable you to grow in a sustainable way.

John Down of The Dots told me that he has a list in his head of what could be delegated, what needs improving and what he wants to keep under his control. Clive Rich of LawBite told me they've started the process of 'marking out every single thing the company does – all the jobs, the responsibilities, all the different constituencies, from soup to nuts'. This will be helpful not just for the next iteration of their software platform but also to identify where they have or need processes.

Operations – Top three takeaways

1. Inconsistency and confusion are completely normal in growing businesses

2. Processes and systems will delight your customers, support your team, save you money and set you free

3. Take a walk in your customer's shoes to understand how easy you are to deal with

CHAPTER EIGHT

Management

'People don't leave bad companies, they leave bad managers.'

— Marcus Buckingham, British author and speaker

It's not uncommon for owners of growing businesses to feel disgruntled about how much work they still have to do, despite a bigger team. They're paying out all this money in salaries and associated costs and yet they're still the one who's in the office late, the one who everyone turns to and wants a piece of, and the one who feels that they're spread too thin and carrying too much. The feeling that all roads still lead to you can be an overwhelming one.

In many small businesses, you'll find the owner on the critical path of all key decisions and projects.

Nothing gets done without their say-so, and many important tasks get held up awaiting their input or approval. These businesses move slowly and are often filled with frustrated people who just want to get on with their jobs.

In the Learning chapter, we looked at how organisations can learn to recognise and embrace mistakes in order to improve and move forward. In businesses where dissent and disagreement aren't tolerated, mistakes are punished, and loyalty is rewarded above honesty, the tendency is for people to stop speaking their mind. 'Yes-men' flourish and so does 'groupthink'. Standards drop as you converge around the lowest common denominator, and paranoia can set in.

Scott Erwin, CEO of Hire Hand, told me that it can be really hard to let go. 'Things are happening that you aren't involved in and maybe don't know about, and that's a really hard moment for a lot of founders. But that's really the moment where you think, "Actually, this thing can almost exist without me, it's something separate from me", and that's quite a moment!'

Many entrepreneurs believe that they have a management team when in reality what they have are senior team members. These people may have been with the company for some time, but they have no real decision-making authority at a company level. They may make decisions on a project or advise more junior team members, but they don't sit around the management table and make decisions about the company, nor do they formally line manage any of the people. In order for your company to grow, this needs to change.

Management – Share the load

Most people who start out in business look for people to get tasks done. Once you've signed up some clients, you need products to ship or services to be performed. Most of the people you're working with will probably be focused on doing. But maybe you're still making most of the decisions yourself. Maybe you expect people to simply step up and take the responsibility without being asked, but perhaps it hasn't occurred to you that they may not necessarily be wired like you (otherwise, they might be off running their own businesses). Ultimately, you're the boss and you need managers around you to share the load.

Richard Royce of LawBite described the process as 'the transition from micromanaging to monitoring', which happens in every business as it grows. For your business, it may happen at seven or eight people, for others, not until twelve or thirteen, but at some point in the growth cycle, you'll need some structure and a management team. In this chapter, we'll look at line management, the art of delegation, how to form an effective management team and how your role as CEO or founder will change as you grow your business.

Line management

A manager, by default, has formal responsibility for managing someone (people) or something (process). A management team is a group of people who manage your business – its people and its processes. If you want to get up and out of the day-to-day running of your business, one of the first steps is sharing the responsibility for managing it. This means collective or distributed decision-making, which can take a bit of getting used to when you've been calling all the shots for a while. However, if you want to grow your business, you'll need a management team.

A line manager is someone who directly manages people and resources in order to achieve team or company goals. Their responsibilities may include the following:

- Providing coaching and constructive performance feedback through regular meetings with each individual
- Communicating team and company goals
- Recruiting and hiring
- Training and supporting
- Monitoring individual and team performance against targets
- Identifying the need for corrective actions

- Reporting on individual and team performance

- Ensuring quality standards

- Working with other line managers to achieve company goals

When you start out in business, everybody will, by default, report to you. There are unlikely to be formal structures in place, which may work well in the early days. But as your team grows, you'll need to think about appointing managers to ensure that your people are properly supported and understand what's expected of them. My view is that every person should have a line manager – someone who's taking an interest in how they are, setting clear expectations and providing coaching and constructive feedback.

The number of people that one person can manage will depend on the experience of the people they're managing, what other responsibilities they have and how much of an impact they want to have on the people they're managing. For most people working in small businesses, where there's so much for everyone to do, trying to manage more than five or six people will be too much. You can supervise more people, but actual management (the list of responsibilities above) will require more of your effort and time. This means that if you have a team of more than five or six, you could already be thinking about handing over line management responsibility to trusted people within your team.

Being a good manager is a skill. Many companies make the mistake of assuming that someone who's good at a particular job will be good at managing people who do that job. It happens all the time – a fantastic salesperson suddenly 'promoted' to sales manager and being out of their depth and feeling like a failure; a talented developer suddenly having to manage a team and ending up with conflict and confusion that they're ill-equipped to deal with. To be a good manager, you don't have to understand or be able to do everything your people do. You need to be able to listen, problem-solve and give feedback.

Becoming a manager for the first time can be daunting, so it's important to have support available for your new managers – mentorship from a more experienced person internally or external support from a coach or advisor. Some new managers struggle to see the value of their role to begin with. If you've spent your life defining your usefulness by how much you achieve, it can be tough to recognise the value of enabling and encouraging other people to get things done.

The art of delegation

One of the most difficult tasks for new managers (and still a challenge for some who are more experienced) is delegation. It can be particularly tough for entrepreneurs who have got used to doing everything to 'let go' of the doing and instead manage others. Often, people think they have delegated, and they may really want to, but in fact, they end up involving others in a process which actually results in their having less time rather than more.

Richard Royce of LawBite explained that he found stepping back and letting go quite hard to begin with. 'Because I know the product the best, I always felt like I was going to be the quickest to look at stuff. Rather than saying "OK, we'll spend two days working out how you can look at this stuff and analyse it," I would spend two hours doing it today, and then I would have a day and a half tomorrow to do something else.' He found making the space and time to do this challenging but recognised that it was necessary for the company to scale.

There are different levels of delegation, and it's a good idea to be clear about what level of control you actually want.

1. Follow these instructions precisely – do exactly as I say.

2. Investigate this, tell me about it and I'll decide.

3. Investigate this, tell me about it and we'll decide together.

4. Tell me what you've found and what you need from me to help you deal with it and then we'll decide.

5. Give me your analysis and recommendations and I'll let you know if you can proceed.

6. You decide – let me know your decision and wait for my approval before proceeding.

7. You decide – let me know your decision and go ahead unless you hear from me.

8. You decide and take action – let me know what you did and what the result was.

9. You decide and take action. You don't need to check back with me.

10. You decide where action needs to be taken and you manage the situation. It's your area of responsibility.

The earlier you are in this list, the more of your time will still be involved. The lower down you go, the more you're empowering the other person to make the decision (and potentially the mistakes). It can be hard to allow mistakes to be made and resolved without you swooping in to save the day. It's a vital skill for any real entrepreneur to develop. If you think you might struggle, ask your people to remind you to 'butt out' if you start poking your nose into something you've clearly delegated.

Here are my top tips on effective delegation.

How to delegate

Effective delegation requires clarity. You must be clear about:

1. The task that you want done

2. The outcome/result that you expect

3. The deadline

4. What the person should do if they get stuck

5. How and when to ask you for guidance or support

6. At what point in the process you want to be consulted or when you want to sign off

7. What to do if things go wrong

Being clear about these seven things will make you a much more effective delegator and the people who are working with you will be very happy if you can give them this level of clarity.

Scott Erwin of Hire Hand has a business model that requires a lot of automation and delegation to facilitate the company's fast growth. He told me, 'The clear thing about automation and outsourcing, quote unquote, from you to members of your team is not sacrificing on quality, but rather trying to understand what parts you can make more efficient without losing the objective. It's quite important to set that standard for the team, have those expectations for your top team, and then you can do things efficiently.'

As you grow and develop your business and continue to delegate more and more, the quality and cost of the people you'll need to fill those roles will increase. As you become more valuable to your business, you need to 'buy back' your time with higher-quality and more capable people.

Management team

A management team is a group of individuals who are responsible for managing the people and the functions of the business. It's responsible for putting together the business strategy and ensuring business objectives are met. The management team is held accountable by the board of directors. This team isn't something that will simply form itself without work. It takes time and effort, and, most importantly, a mindset shift by the business owner.

In many family-run businesses, management teams can form over many years without much clarity around roles and responsibilities and decision processes. Paul and Julia Whyte of Whyte & Co told me about trying to get the balance right between clear lines of responsibility and trust between all parties, and how a group of people can learn to work harmoniously together. They're revamping their role profiles and ensuring greater clarity around roles and responsibilities, which they believe will help them continue to sustain their business.

Here are my top tips for forming your effective management team.

Your management team

1. **Structure.** As your business grows, you'll need to professionalise its structure. That spaghetti organisational chart will need to be streamlined. Instead of thinking about the people, think about the company. Depending on your business, you may have a product development or tech team, and you'll certainly have some sort of a commercial team (sales, business development, etc.). Thinking about the functions of your business can be helpful – put the people aside for the time being (find out more about organisational structures in the Further Reading section). Ask yourself, *'What are the main activities in our business? How could they be grouped?'*

2. **People.** Once you're clearer about the structure your business needs, you can start thinking about the people. You need a diverse mix of people, with different perspectives and strengths, who will collaborate but also challenge each other. Ask yourself, *'Who are the leaders? Who has the knowledge and also the desire to step up and take on more responsibility? Who would make good decisions on behalf of the company?'*

3. **Engage.** This step is often missed – ask people whether they want to be a manager. It's not for everyone. Describe your planned structure, get inputs and ask individuals whether they want a seat at the table. This process has to be handled delicately. Some will feel left out, others may feel insecure – it's not your job to keep everyone happy but to provide clarity. Keep your communication honest, factual and as transparent as you can. Ask yourself, *'Who do I need to talk to? What am I asking and telling each person?'*

4. **Convene.** Bring your new management team together and get each person to map out the roles and responsibilities of their new position. Get everyone's input to ensure that no area of the business is missing. The principle is that all significant tasks performed within your business should be represented by someone around that table. Ask yourself, *'When do I want this process to start? How will it be managed?'*

5. **Communication.** Inform the whole team of the new structure, roles and responsibilities. Make sure you give your people the opportunity to ask questions. The decision may have been made, but people still need to feel listened to and heard. Ask yourself, *'What is my plan to communicate this change? Who may need to be handled beforehand?'*

6. **Collaboration.** For collective responsibility to work effectively, your management team will need to build up trust over time. Honest and open

communication will be vital, as will constructive feedback. All decisions that are made should be owned by someone in the room at the time. If you need someone else to do something, someone in the room should take the action to speak with that person and report back. Ask yourself, *'How do I ensure that we are collaborating openly? How will I know if we trust each other?'*

7. **Incentives.** I believe that management teams should feel absolutely responsible for the management of the business, so I'm an advocate of ensuring that a portion of each person's compensation is tied to the specific goals of the business. Ask yourself, *'What incentives am I prepared to offer my management team?'*

8. **Empowerment.** Once you've set up your management team, you must make sure that its members remain empowered to make decisions. This means backing them in front of your team and your customers. If you undermine your managers by overruling them or allowing your team to go over their managers' heads, you'll continue to find that all roads lead back to you. Make sure that disagreements with your managers are handled behind closed doors and that decisions are communicated to the broader team in a clear and transparent manner. Ask yourself, *'Is my management team taking the decisions they are supposed to be? Am I letting go enough?'*

This process will take time and effort and you may well make mistakes as you go. On the difficult days, remember what you are trying to achieve and *why*.

Structure

Every company has slightly different needs, but many find that a heads-of-department approach to forming their management team works well.

Julian Cork, COO of Landbay, told me that they recently implemented such a structure, where each of their 'heads' is responsible for the individual projects in their area with key organisational decisions and priorities being made by the senior management team. The driver behind this structure was the need for greater transparency and to help the teams focus and allocate resources effectively and avoid everything being a priority. John Goodall, Landbay's CEO, made the point that some areas of their business are more suited to hierarchy than others and that they were keen to have enough structure while retaining the agility, flexibility and quick decision-making of a start-up, to differentiate themselves from other lenders.

John Down of The Dots told me that they take to heart the Facebook model of 'never more than four layers of governance from Mark Zuckerberg'. He said that it all depends on the calibre of people you bring into your business. 'Some people need hierarchy. They're probably not appropriate for this type of business. We need people who are happy with being self-starters with a level of ambiguity as well as doing what needs to be done.'

The role of the CEO

Ultimately, as the owner and director of your business, your job is to do the right thing for that business. One of the hardest things for any business owner is to recognise when it's time for their role to change.

At the start of every business is an idea usually accompanied by a burst of energy and enthusiasm, a vision of the future and a desire for change. This instinctive, impatient and future-focused energy is what the business needs in order to start. Without it, little would get off the ground, which is why so many business owners have it in abundance. But as your business evolves, the very energy that was essential at the start becomes less useful and may even become destructive if not properly channelled. This is because the creative instinct is to want variety and renewal, and as your business becomes more of a 'machine', change isn't necessarily what's needed. This is why many successful companies keep their creator's energies focused on strategy and looking to the future, where change and new ideas are valuable, and keep them away from operations and delivery, where consistency and certainty are essential (but anathema to very creative people).

As businesses grow and structures and processes get established with a strong management team in place, some founders find themselves struggling to define their role. Are you still the right person to lead your organisation? What types of people does it really need? If your business could choose, what role would it have you playing over the coming months and years?

This can be a painful process for some founders. Many experience guilt if they spend any time away from the business. Others don't think it's fair to ask their team to work harder or longer hours than they do. The truth is that this is about quality and not quantity. To get some perspective on your business, you need to take time away from it. Rather than harming your business, your being refreshed, energised and clear-headed will only improve it. Your job as a business owner is to do the right thing for your business, and that might be taking time out to come up with new strategies or products. It might be handing over significant control to others more suited to the roles you've previously held.

It can be awkward to move from 'doing' to 'being the boss'. It's a change of identity, a change in how you and others see you and your role. Many entrepreneurs have their identity so tightly tied up in their business that however hard they try, they cannot step 'up and out'. Your job is to ask yourself, *'What's the next block that needs removing from my business?'* and then remove it. Be open to the possibility that there may come a day when that block is you.

Management – Top three takeaways

1. A management team is responsible for the people and functions of the company

2. Different levels of delegation require more or less of your time and give you more or less control

3. Management is more about listening than telling

CHAPTER NINE

Metrics

'If you can't measure it, you can't improve it.'

— Peter Drucker, Austrian-born writer on
management theory and practice

If you put the above quote into any search engine, you'll find a large number of opinion pieces which range from almost slavish agreement to downright indignation from people who, quite correctly, point out that you can't measure everything. However, if we put Drucker's quote into context by pairing it with another of his most famous utterances, 'Management is doing things right; leadership is doing the right thing', we get a sense that measuring the right things is an important aspect of managing our businesses.

Metrics can appear deceptively simple or devilishly complex, and the danger is that information without context can drive decisions and behaviours that you may not be able to predict. Simply put, without measuring the critical elements of your business, you and your management team have no way of knowing what state the business is in, what direction it's heading in and whether it's on track or falling behind. If the data you're looking at is confused, ill-defined or inaccurate, it may lead to poor alignment and decisions as well as missed opportunities.

Poor cash-flow management brings many businesses to their knees. People have a myriad of attitudes and relationships with money, which can make it a challenge to manage. For some people, money is linked to self-worth. Money heavily influences our attitude towards risk, work and how we manage our lives and our businesses. A lot of people don't enjoy looking at numbers, and many believe that they're not good with finances, and so this is an area that's often over-delegated.

Our attitude to money clearly impacts our ability to run our businesses, and this is particularly true in the early stages of a business, when you're trying to figure out what your products and services are and what they're worth. A common mistake is to set prices too low because you're desperate for business. Your product or service needs to be positioned at a level where you can make enough margin to cover your costs with a decent buffer – your customers won't thank you if you have to raise prices later on. Don't be afraid to invest in quality, especially when it comes to people and products, but make sure you're all over your numbers and really clear about what you're measuring. The balance between prudence and quality is something that every entrepreneur needs to figure out.

Not all surprises are good. Many entrepreneurs think they have a good handle on what's going on in their business. But every now and then, they get an uncomfortable feeling in their gut because they realise they don't. What most will do when this happens is talk to a few people and ask them what they think. The result is subjective opinions based on assumptions with some bias, egos and conflicting agendas thrown in for good measure. It's important to hear what people have to say, but facts are a vital counterbalance if you want to really know what's going on in your business.

Metrics – Measure what's important

A good scorecard helps your team work on the right things, measure performance against projections and goals and spot trends and stay ahead. Remember that it's not what you measure that's important but the meaning you give that measurement.

Some entrepreneurs try to measure everything and some don't measure anything at all. Too much data can be just as bad as too little – the challenge is deciding what the truly important metrics are. Many people set out with good intentions to construct a meaningful scorecard to help them manage their businesses, only to find that they have taken their eye off what really matters. In this chapter, we'll look at the rhythm of your business, how to build a scorecard for your business, how to manage your cash flow and how to assess your competitive advantage.

Business rhythm

In the Resilience section of this book, we looked at how to establish a healthy routine for yourself. Businesses develop their own rhythms, often influenced by their customers' needs – you learn quickly when there will be demand for your products and services and you build your team accordingly. As you grow, you'll need to develop a rhythm for managing your business. This means getting clear about what activities need to happen weekly, monthly, quarterly and annually.

These will vary depending on the size of your team and the nature of your business, but here's a structure to get you thinking about what will work for you and your people.

The rhythm of your business

1. **Management Meeting (Weekly)** – Brief session (no more than an hour) every week to review the key

actions, decisions and any burning issues. These meetings need to be well-facilitated and to the point.

2. **Management Meeting (Monthly)** – Typically a two- to three-hour session to review key metrics and the important but not urgent issues you are tracking such as personnel changes and budget pressures.

3. **Management Meeting (Quarterly)** – To review progress against plan, typically a full day or two half days.

4. **Management Meeting (Annual)** – To set strategy and targets for the year ahead. Try and do this one away from the office and take at least a full day.

5. **Team Meeting (Weekly)** – Each team or function within your business has a regular meeting, usually weekly, short and sweet, between thirty minutes and one hour depending on the size of the team. When you're small, some functions will only be one person in which case it will be a one-to-one (see below). These sessions are held to ensure that everyone in each function or team is on the same page, understands what the challenges are and can work together to solve any problems. These departmental meetings escalate any decisions they cannot take within the team to the Weekly Management Meeting.

6. **One-to-One Meeting** – It's really important that every person in your business has a formal line

manager who holds a regular meeting with them. Weekly is great but at least monthly is advised. The purpose of these sessions is for the individual to be able to share any concerns they have, receive feedback and get coaching on their role. Career aspirations and any conflict situations are also discussed during these sessions. In small growing businesses, these meetings are often skipped on the grounds that you all see each other all the time. However, I would not underestimate the power of these regular conversations. People will tell you things they would not otherwise 'bother you with' if you make the time to sit with them one on one.

7. **Whole Company Meeting (Quarterly)** – Get the whole company together to review the results from the previous quarter and align everyone to the challenges and opportunities of the year ahead.

8. **Whole Company Meeting (Annual)** – At the beginning of each financial year, get your whole company together to share the strategy and targets for the year. Do this away from the office if you can and include some team building activities.

It's vital to get your full team together regularly so that everyone receives the same messages. When you start out, it's relatively easy to keep everyone informed, but I would still recommend getting everyone together regularly. Many entrepreneurs underestimate the desire people have to know what's going on. As I've said, your job is not to make everyone happy but to give everyone clarity. Here are some questions to ask yourself:

- *'How do we structure our management meetings? What do we cover in each?'*

- *'Which functional meetings do we run? How do they feed up into management meetings?'*

- *'How often do we hold one-to-ones with our people? How effective are they?'*

- *'How often do we get our whole team together? What do we cover in these sessions?'*

Effective meetings

Meetings are an essential part of making decisions, agreeing accountabilities and running a business. Unfortunately, too many meetings are long, boring and pointless. Here are seven golden rules for ensuring that your meetings are productive and valuable to all who attend.

1. **Clear objectives.** All meetings must have a defined purpose and a specific desired outcome. Be clear what you are looking to accomplish. Are you communicating a change, looking for input or wanting to make a decision? Meetings with no clear purpose are generally a waste of time. Add the objective to your agenda and restate it at the

beginning of the session so that all attendees are aware and can contribute to achieving it.

2. **Attendees.** Before you invite anyone, think about who actually needs to be there. Who will be affected by the changes you are announcing, who can help you fix the issues or who needs to be involved in the decisions. If people don't feel that they can contribute or be useful they will not see the meeting as a good use of their time. Make sure you and all attendees are adequately prepared. For meetings where important decisions will be made, this may mean a one-on-one discussion with some key individuals prior to the meeting to ensure that they are fully briefed on what needs to happen.

3. **Agenda.** Have an agenda and stick to it. Everything on your agenda should contribute directly to achieving the objective of the meeting – leave out anything that doesn't. Think about how much time is required for each topic, consider the most appropriate sequence and who should lead each topic. Lay out what you plan to cover in the meeting, including time slots. Add the date, time and location, and email it to the attendees and any deputies in advance. Make it clear what's expected of attendees, including any preparation that may be required. Print out copies for the meeting or put it up on a screen to help keep people on track. Always run through the actions from the last meeting so everyone has context

but also people are more likely to complete their actions if they know you are going to ask them for an update.

4. **Clear ground rules.** Be clear about the rules, especially those around decision-making. Ensure that people understand what decisions will be made in your meetings and that they must send a fully empowered deputy if they're unable to attend. Don't get yourself in a situation where people do not support the decisions made in your meetings because they chose not to attend. Do not allow technology in your meetings – you want people fully present or not at all. Start on time and finish on time, people will appreciate that you value their time and will soon learn that your meetings are a good use of it.

5. **Facilitation.** Keep the meeting on track by being firm and keeping calm. Keep an eye on the clock, remind people of the allocated time so that they stay conscious of what's happening. If you need to stop someone talking too much or taking the meeting off track, then do so politely but firmly (see also Rule 6). Ask other people for their inputs, especially those who aren't contributing. Bring people back to the agenda and objectives of the meeting. Stay in control but take feedback and inputs. All actions should be captured with a specific deliverable or output, a single owner (who is in the room) and a committed timeline. At the end of each topic make a quick summary and

confirm action items. Ask participants to confirm that your summary is correct. Five minutes before the end of the meeting, quickly summarise the key points and agree next steps, including the date and time of the next meeting. Do not wait until people start leaving.

6. **The 'Parking Lot'.** A really useful tool where you capture important points that are 'off-topic'. This allows you to acknowledge the importance of these points while keeping your meeting on track. Make sure that you let people know you will be using this device in order to keep the meeting focused. It is very important that you include these points in your follow-up (see Rule 7) along with next steps.

7. **Follow up.** Make sure you document the key decisions, actions (including owners), parking lot topics and next steps from the meeting and circulate it to the participants and impacted stakeholders. I always try to do this within 24 hours of the meeting. Give people a specific amount of time to send feedback or contributions, after which your notes become the agreed record of the meeting.

Improving the quality of meetings takes effort. It is important to challenge what you do and how on a regular basis to ensure that you are making the best use of everybody's time.

Building a business scorecard

To run the business effectively, you and your management team need to be able to judge its health using data. I highly recommend creating a one-page view of your business at least once a month. So how do you construct this document and what information should it contain?

Scorecard tool

1. **Define metrics.** As your business grows, you'll need to focus on different metrics. When you start out, you're likely to be focused on **revenue**, **cash** and **burn rates**, but as you scale, other metrics will become important. **Conversion rates** and number of **leads** will need your focus as you grow, and then, as you become more established, **utilisation** and **efficiency** will start to take priority. These may vary from business to business and between industries, but here are some other metrics to think about:

   a. **Margin** – arguably the most important, as it reflects the bottom line. Clearly your revenue must exceed your cost of goods sold (costs directly attributable to sales, eg raw materials and variable costs) and your operating expenses (rent, salaries, fixed costs, etc.) in order for you to be able to afford to stay in business for any length of time. Your gross margin is calculated by subtracting your cost of goods sold from your revenue, which gives you your gross profit, and then dividing that by your revenue. This number is how much you have left to pay your operating expenses. Your net margin is calculated by deducting all costs from revenue to get net profit and then dividing that by your revenue. This is how much true profit your company is making.

b. **Retention** - looks at the percentage of customers that stay with you. There are several ways to calculate it, depending on your business model, but probably the simplest way is to subtract the number of new customers from your total customers at the end of each period (week, month, quarter – whatever makes sense in your business), and then divide that by the number of customers you started the period with. The goal is to keep this retention rate as high as possible.

c. **Customer acquisition cost (CAC)** - pick a specific time period and divide your cost of marketing and sales by the number of customers you gained. What 'good' looks like will depend on your business model and industry, but generally the lower the better. A rising CAC can be a problem, but not if you've just introduced a new product or service with a higher margin. Like most data, you need to track it over time and look at it in context along with other metrics.

   d. **Customer lifetime revenue** – looks at the
   revenue you receive from repeat customers. It
   can be difficult to measure in the early days,
   but as you gather more data, you can start
   making some assumptions. Knowing your
   customer lifetime revenue is important, as it
   helps you assess how much you can afford in
   CAC (see above).

   e. **Return on advertising spend** – divide your
   sales by the advertising spend associated with
   those sales. While simple to figure out, this
   number can be misleading if you're marketing
   across channels. Make sure you're gathering
   meaningful data before using it to drive
   decisions.

2. **Set targets.** Each metric should have a target
   which is tracked monthly, quarterly or annually,
   depending on what's appropriate.

3. **Define owners.** Each metric should have an owner
   around the management team table.

4. **Track.** Have someone compile the scorecard in
   advance of your management meeting.

5. **Review.** I recommend reviewing your
   management scorecard monthly.

6. **Take action.** As a management team, you'll need
   to decide what actions to take as a result of your
   review of the scorecard.

As you grow, you may wish to have each department or division of your business replicate the meeting and scorecard structure described above. The responsible managers of each team can report up to divisional meetings, which in turn report to the senior management meeting. Getting the balance right between structure and flexibility, ensuring that information flows as needed without unnecessary bureaucracy, is one of the key challenges that all real entrepreneurs wrestle with as their businesses grow.

Objectives and key results

Many companies, such as Google, Intel, LinkedIn and Twitter, use a framework to define and track objectives and outcomes called objectives and key results (OKR). The main benefit of such a framework is it keeps the team and individuals focused on objectives which align with the company's vision and goals.

Pip Jamieson told me that they use OKRs at The Dots because simply focusing on hitting achievable Key Performance Indicators (KPIs) or targets isn't enough for them. 'If we want to be the biggest professional network in the world, we also want the team to be thinking about that goal as a part of their role, innovating and achieving that big-level vision.' As companies scale, it's not uncommon for people lower down in the organisation to have little or no idea how what they're doing contributes to what the company is looking to achieve, and without that *why*, it's easy to become demotivated or start simply going through the motions. OKRs are designed to keep everyone aligned and focused. Because they empower the team more than KPIs do, everyone has a say in how things get built, which removes some of the pressure from the founders' and senior management's shoulders.

How to implement OKRs

OKRs are usually straightforward to implement and track. Here's how.

1. **Objectives** – Define three to five key objectives at company, team or personal level. They should be ambitious, qualitative, time bound and actionable by a person or team.

2. **Results** – Under each objective, define three to five measurable results. They should be quantifiable, objective and challenging. OKR results can be based on revenue, growth, performance or engagement. They're usually numerical but can also be binary (1 or 0).

3. **Communicate** – Once the structure of the OKRs has been established, they need to be communicated to the whole team, which might involve some tuning of language so that everyone understands what they mean.

4. **Update** – Each person is responsible for updating their OKRs, usually weekly. According to the OKR framework, an objective is considered done

when 70 to 75% of its results have been achieved. If 100% is achieved, the objective isn't ambitious enough and is usually revised.

5. **Review** – OKRs are flexible and should be changed according to the reality of your business. The point is to keep your people working on ambitious goals rather than insignificant tasks.

OKRs are usually reviewed formally on a quarterly basis. It's important to understand that OKRs aren't related to performance. As Pip Jamieson told me, 'It's all about the team shooting for the vision. You're not actually meant to achieve that vision. Sometimes you do and it's wonderful.' For example, if your vision is to have 0% churn or turnover of clients, you're unlikely to ever achieve that, but it will lead the team to take different actions than if people are focused on a KPI of 10% churn. For insights into how OKRs were introduced to Google and many other successful businesses, take a look at *Measure What Matters: OKRs – The Simple Idea that Drives 10x Growth* by John Doerr (Penguin, 2018).

Whichever method you choose, if you don't measure the progress you're making, or the gap between your vision and your reality, you risk becoming frustrated. Measuring helps you stay out of the gap. If you don't have objective measures in place, you risk making decisions based on false information, and this will quickly erode the trust people have in your judgement and that of your management team.

Ensure you put metrics in place to measure the important aspects of your business, so that you know your management team is dealing with facts and not just best guesses or what people tell you. If someone is always telling you that everything is fine, be wary. In business, something is usually breaking – that's the way we learn and grow. Accountability means encouraging people to be open and honest about failures as well as successes.

Managing cash flow

Even when businesses have healthy revenue and profit, it's not unusual for them to face cash-flow challenges, especially in the early days. A simple rolling ten- to twelve-week forecast will keep your finger on the pulse. Many owner-managers delegate the management of their finances early on, perhaps because they don't feel comfortable with numbers or because they think it's more important to focus on customers and products. But if you don't keep a close eye on the numbers, you risk not being able to survive to enjoy the growth you're working so hard to achieve.

Here are some tips for keeping the cash flowing:

- Make sure you have someone in your organisation you can trust to keep an eye on the numbers and keep you up to speed.

- Invoice upfront if you can (at least for a portion of your work).

- Get a standing order set up for future payments.

- Set a credit limit for each customer, and get a process in place to warn them when they get close to their limit; advise that they need to pay your invoice to be able to order more.

- Include late-payment interest terms on your invoice and offer your customer the option to pay early to avoid the interest charge.

- If you offer warranties or extra services, state in your terms and conditions that these don't apply if invoices aren't paid on time.

- Know when the payment runs of your customers are, and start chasing in time to hit them.

- Use coloured envelopes to ensure that your invoices are noticed. If you send your invoices by email, but post reminders, then ensure these are sent in coloured envelopes or on coloured paper.

- Include a small chocolate or something similar in the envelope – it will make you memorable.

- Build up a relationship with your customer's accounts payable team.

- When you send an end-of-year gift or card, don't forget the person who pays the invoices.

Here are some questions to get you thinking about how to manage cash flow in your business:

- *'Do you have someone in your business who's looking at cash flow (not your accountant!)?'*
- *'Do you have a cash-flow budget for this year and do you know where your business is against it?'*
- *'Do you have clear payment terms and is performance against those monitored in your business?'*
- *'Do you invoice quickly after a job is finished?'*
- *'Do you offer retainer packages to your clients?'*
- *'Do you have a diverse customer base and does it have low turnover?'*
- *'Do you know how much there is in your business bank account this month?'*

Assessing competitive advantage

The VRIO (value, rarity, imitability, organisation) model is a quick and easy way to look at the resources of any business and assess its competitive advantage. In essence, it's about asking 'What makes my business unique?' It might be the strength of your brand, the quality of your leadership or team, your well-managed processes and strong finances, or your global presence and partnerships.

We start with looking at the **value** that each resource adds to the organisation – does it help the firm exploit opportunities or defend against threats? Does it increase perceived customer value? If you can answer yes, then you have a competitive advantage.

Next, we look at **rarity**. How difficult would it be for competitors to leverage the same resources as you? If your resources are rare, you may have a temporary competitive advantage, but even being on parity with access to the same resources isn't necessarily a problem if you can deploy them more creatively or efficiently.

Then, we look at **imitability**. Can your resources be duplicated and substituted? There may be historical reasons why your resources are difficult to copy – for example, resources that take a long time to develop – or your advantage may be that your resources are difficult to identify and therefore imitate, like a secret recipe. As well, some organisations have intangible aspects that can be hard to imitate, such as culture and relationships.

Finally, we look at how a business is **organised** in order to capture the value of its resources. As we saw in the Operations chapter, having the wrong business model may seriously impact your ability to maintain competitive advantage. You need to be organised to maximise the resources that you have – the right management processes, systems, policies and culture.

So how do you use the VRIO model and what might it mean for your business?

Applying the VRIO model

Step One – Identify resources that are valuable, rare and difficult or costly to imitate. These may be physical assets but are more likely to be intangible resources such as brand reputation, trademarks, and unique methods and processes.

Step Two – Organise – Determine how well your business is set up to exploit these resources to their full potential. What are your retention policies? What kind of management controls do you have in place?

Step Three – Protect – You'll need to prioritise which resources to protect. Those that have all four VRIO attributes should be protected at all costs, as they're the source of your competitive advantage. Think about how to make them more costly to imitate, so they keep the rarity factor longer.

Step Four – Review your VRIO resources and capabilities regularly (if you're in a competitive situation, at least quarterly). The value of resources is constantly changing, so you'll need to have strategies in place to avoid competitors moving against you.

Metrics – Top three takeaways

1. You can move only what you measure

2. Create a rhythm for managing your business

3. Trust your gut, but have the facts to guide you

Bringing Accountability together

Accountability is all about providing clarity – for your team, customers, suppliers and investors. What are you building, what does 'good' look like and what is the best way to deliver value? It's about building the 'machine' that delivers and will continue to deliver to your customers in a high-quality and consistent way. Try to see your business through their eyes. How would you feel if you were a customer of your business? How special is your business really, and is it set up to efficiently and predictably delight your customers while outperforming your competitors? Take time to focus on the key metrics in your business. What are the levers that can be pulled to effect meaningful change? To build the necessary structures and provide effective management for all your people, you'll need to find a team of trusted individuals to step up and share the load with you. Once you find them, you need to empower them to take the decisions that need to be taken. To be a real entrepreneur, you need to put in place the right people and processes so that your business can thrive.

- What are your key takeaways from the Accountability section?

- What are you going to implement immediately?

- What are you looking at differently now?

PART FOUR

L IS FOR LEADERSHIP

Leadership isn't about being the most senior in the room. Successful and ambitious companies are looking to encourage leadership behaviours at all levels. One of my favourite stories about leadership is from the time of the moon landings. The US president of the day, John F Kennedy, was visiting NASA when he spotted a man mopping the floor. Legend has it that he walked up to him, shook his hand and asked him what his job was. The man looked at him and said, 'I help put man on moon.' Can you imagine if your team, all of your team, were that engaged with the mission of your company? If Resilience is the heart of our business, Energy its life blood and Accountability its structure, then Leadership is the driving force that moves it forward. Leadership is the final pillar of the REAL model®, bringing the cycle and focus back round to you and how you want to show up in your business.

If you feel that people in your business are pulling in different directions, if you regularly change your mind about what the focus should be and if you struggle to keep good people, then this section is where to start. If there's a lot of activity but little team spirit, this section will show you how to galvanise your team towards a shared purpose. If the priorities are unclear, and firefighting becomes the norm, then people will feel confused, momentum will fade and conflict will increase. This section will help you decide what kind of leader you want to be, as well as how to focus on encouraging leadership throughout your business.

Leadership starts with having a clear and compelling vision that you share with your team and the people around you. You need to build towards that vision with a well-thought-out plan while staying true to your values and the values of the business.

CHAPTER TEN

Vision

'Leadership is the capacity to translate vision into reality.'

— Warren G. Bennis, American pioneer in the study of leadership

At the heart of most business or development training is the idea that to get what you want, you have to do something – you have to take action. It's also the most common advice given by experts across the world. To achieve, we need to do something. And yet most people fail to do so, even though we all instinctively understand that it works. If you dig into the reasons why people fail to take action, you'll find that we're usually taking plenty of actions but not necessarily the ones that will enable us to achieve our goals. At the core of this problem is the fact that most people don't really know what they want. If you don't have a clear vision, you'll spend your time taking actions that don't get you where you want to be.

When a company doesn't have a clear vision, the same thing happens. It ambles along with no energy or purpose. It's uninspiring and likely to fail. In these kinds of companies, everyone makes up their own mind about which direction they're heading in and what kind of business is being created. We've all seen businesses that seem to switch focus on a regular basis – restructuring is a favourite distraction that some businesses rely on regularly.

If you're not attracting the people you want to your business, it may be because your vision isn't clear enough or bold enough. The bigger, more ambitious, bolder your vision and plans, the more you'll attract high-calibre people to you and your business. Conversely, if your vision isn't consistent, you risk losing your best people to someone whose is.

Vision – Go for what you want

If you're struggling with lack of motivation despite making progress and looking after yourself, you may be suffering from a lack of vision. Having a goal isn't enough. Try to think beyond the goal: What will you do with the money when you make it? What gets you out of bed every morning? If you can't answer the *why* question, your goals aren't going to be very motivating. Juliet Eccleston of AnyGood? told me that people are starting to approach her because they believe in the vision and what her and her co-founder Carl are looking to do to disrupt the recruitment industry – people want to be a part of it.

Simon Sinek, the author of *Start with Why: How Great Leaders Inspire Everyone to Take Action* (Penguin, 2011), believes that very few people or businesses can clearly articulate why they do what they do, and that 'we are drawn to people and organisations that are good at communicating what they believe'.

In the early days of Microsoft, Bill Gates, founder and then CEO, gave his company its mission: 'A computer on every desk and in every home.' The great companies of our age continue to have bold and inspirational visions. Amazon exists so that 'customers can find and discover anything they might want to buy online', while Facebook wants to 'bring the world closer together' and Google aims 'to provide access to the world's information in one click'. In this section, we'll look at how to get to the heart of vision and how to craft a vibrant vision that will galvanise people.

Getting to the heart of vision

Do you remember all the media interest when a passenger got dragged off a United Airlines flight? There was such a lot of attention and so many questions being asked that the CEO had to go on TV and do a 'mea culpa' interview. Nobody had ever seen him before – they had no idea who he was. How different would that have been if it had been Richard

Branson? We all think we know him. Most people like and probably trust him. Many of us would have been prepared to forgive him. While this example references the power of personality, the point is that your company starts with you. People want to know who you are, what your purpose is and why you do what you do. It's possible to build a brand without it being centred around you but it's increasingly difficult to differentiate your business without including some aspects of you as the founder.

One of the most interesting parts of the interviews that I conducted when writing this book was hearing people talking about their vision and why they do what they do. I first heard Scott Erwin of Hire Hand speak at a fundraising event, and when he talked about the 'dignity of work', the hairs on the back of my neck stood up. When I interviewed him, he explained, '[Many entrepreneurs] see themselves as cycling through multiple businesses because they love the life cycle of creating a business, making it into something or other, or there's something about the lifestyle of that world. There are others that just get sucked in by a problem, looking around to see if anyone is dealing with it. You find yourself drawn, just because you feel like it's just calling you and it's something that you can't ignore.' He told me that the problem he saw in the market 'got under his skin' and he felt that he had to look at it.

Many founders have this sense of being drawn to what they do, as if it's a compulsion or a need. This passion is one of the things that gets them through those days when nothing works and everything feels too difficult.

Ikigai - Finding your why

The Japanese concept of ikigai roughly translates as 'a reason for being'. Each one of us has an ikigai, but it can be quite a journey to discover it. The Ikigai model is four interlocking circles.

1. Start with what you're good at – what strengths, skills, experience do you have?

2. Next, what do you love – what really drives and motivates you?

At the intersection of these two circles is your *passion*.

3. The third circle is what the world needs – what do you feel compelled to change in the world?

At the intersection of what you love and what the world needs is your *mission*.

4. The fourth circle is what you can get paid for – what is worth money?

At the intersection of what you can get paid for and what the world needs is your *vocation*, and at the intersection of what you can get paid for and what you're good at is your *profession*.

In the centre of these four interlocking circles is your *ikigai*. It's easy to get tempted by all the things we could do, and it's a huge privilege to live in an age where so much is possible, but ikigai helps us focus on what we feel drawn to do. Whenever things get tough in business, and they often do, a foundation of *why* we do what we do serves as a stabilising force to keep us on track. Not every business is closely aligned with its founder's ikigai, but the more closely it is, the more likely you are to stick with it and make it a success.

Even if you spend most of your time in the day-to-day, it's vital that you take time to step 'up and out' every now and then to remind yourself of why you do what you do. The clearer you can get on this, the more of the right resources you'll be able to attract. In the Further Reading section of this book, I've included a link to a video on YouTube – comedian Michael Junior demonstrating in a beautiful and eloquent way the power of finding your why. Connecting to your life's purpose will bring your work and your business onto a whole other level of existence, where you can speak your truth and play to your strengths.

Crafting a vibrant vision

A carefully crafted vision statement is at the heart of every successful business, large or small. Your vision statement must clearly and concisely communicate your business's overall goals and be used to support decision-making across your business as part of your strategic plan. It describes your company's ambition and its vision for the future. It can be as simple as one sentence, or much longer, but must define the core ideals that shape your business (the *why*). An effective vision statement can be a powerful communication tool that helps to empower and motivate your team, and it's likely to contribute to higher levels of alignment, engagement and, therefore, productivity. Given the impact that a strong vision can have on the success of your business, it's worth taking the time to craft a powerful statement with your management team, taking inputs from your key stakeholders.

Vision statements speak about the future to give a clear sense of where the business is going and what it will achieve. They're designed to inspire and give direction to your team on the journey towards the company's goals. They give the team a sense of common purpose and unity as they work together. You can't do this alone – it's about galvanising the energy of the people in your organisation so that they become catalysts for action. The good news is that there's a definite shift towards people wanting to work for a company that has a vision they can align and engage with. For the real entrepreneur who's clear about why they're building the business that they are, there will be no shortage of people who want to align themselves with the future that you're describing. If you can get your people really bought in, there's no end to what you can achieve.

So how do you go about creating a really strong vision statement that your people can align themselves with? Here's a tool that I use.

Vision statement tool

Your vision statement should:

- Use clear and concise language

- Be no longer than a few sentences – something that's meaningful for every member of your team (not just your management team)

- Include big, bold goals and aspirations – five or ten years into the future

- Align with your core brand values and be filled with passion and emotion

- Align with the impact you want to make on the world and your picture of success, regardless of how impractical you think it might be!

- Be as specific, distinct and challenging as possible – generic goals usually lead to mediocre results

Here are the four steps.

1. **Define what you do.** Focus on the outcomes of what your company does. For example, a dressmaker makes dresses, but the outcome is happy customers wearing those dresses. This may sound simple but can actually be a

profound process to go through with your team. *'What do we do?'*

2. **Determine what's unique about the way you deliver that outcome.** Very few products and services are truly unique – most are a different approach or a reinvention of something that exists already. Consider our dressmaker. What makes their dresses special? Is it the material or the design? *'What makes our way special?'*

3. **Quantify.** Who are you targeting? Every single potential customer? Everybody within your local area? What types of customers? Try to add something measurable into your vision, like a number or a timeline. *'Who do we specifically want to serve?'*

4. **Add something relatable.** The key here is something that will spark the imagination – put a picture into the mind of anyone reading your vision. For example, our dressmaker could include a reference to people leaving their shop smiling. This is better than using the word 'happy' because now we're actually picturing someone smiling as they walk out in a new fabulous dress. This might not always be possible, depending on your business, but try to get something 'real' in there if you can. *'How do we want people to feel when they experience our products or services?'*

So, our dressmaker's vision statement could look something like this: 'Producing custom-made dresses with a vintage twist that are so fabulous that every customer who wears one does so with a smile.' There are many ways to craft a strong vision statement, and even if yours doesn't end up looking like this example, following these four steps will help you bring structure and purpose to the process.

Leadership starts with having a clear vision and leading from the front. In his classic book *The Art of War* (LBA, 2019), Sun Tzu declares that 'a leader leads by example, not by force'. Your people will follow you if they believe in you. Scott Erwin of Hire Hand told me that it's a huge advantage when your team buys into the vision: 'People respond to a large problem or social mission, rather than simply the pursuit of profit.'

Vision – Top three takeaways

1. Your job is not to make everyone happy but to provide them with clarity

2. Your people will align with a strong and purposeful vision

3. Lead by example

CHAPTER ELEVEN

Values

'Values provide perspective in the best of times and the worst.'

— Charles Garfield, American author and speaker

Values and culture are often confused. Values guide decision-making. They give us a sense of what's important and what's right. Culture is the combination of business practices, processes and the way we do things, or, as Herb Kelleher, former CEO of Southwest Airlines, is quoted as saying, 'Culture is what people do when no one is looking.' If you find yourself having what feels like a disproportionately strong reaction to something that seems insignificant to others, you're probably experiencing your values being crossed.

A company's values don't change often. They are the uncompromising core principles that a company is prepared to stand by. Its culture, on the other hand, is a constantly evolving landscape that sits on top of its values. It adapts to the business's needs as well as those of its environment and the demands of its customers.

In a study conducted by Facebook, and referenced in several articles, including one published by the Harvard Business Review in January 2018, poor leadership and badly crafted roles were cited as the main reasons people leave their jobs. Poor internal communication, lack of team spirit and micromanagement are all potential signs of a negative company culture. Increased tension and too much competition can also be symptoms. Too much focus on the bottom line and short-term returns have been shown to contribute to a weak culture (see links in the Further Reading section).

If your values aren't clear, well communicated and understood, you risk bringing in the wrong people. If you find that you're regularly hiring people who don't fit in with the company's culture and ways of working, who don't get on with other team members or who behave in ways you find unacceptable, you need to focus on defining values for your business that resonate with you and your team. If it feels as if your team is going through the motions and nobody's heart is really in the job, another look at your values might be in order.

Values – Speak your truth

People are tribal by nature. We define ourselves in terms of our gender, race, age, nationality, religion, sex, beliefs, opinions, etc., and we're drawn to those with whom we have interests or people 'in common'. We also define ourselves by what we are not. We learn at a young age about groups, cliques, gangs – how to fit in and how to stand out. Throughout history, millions of people have been slaughtered in the name of the tribe, and today's politics show us that tribalism is still alive and well. That sense of belonging is incredibly important for most people, and who they work for is no exception. People want to feel a sense of connection with the company, its mission and values, and its people.

Values matter in business. Every successful company has a set of values that assist their team in achieving their goals. They are the essence of the company's identity and why it does what it does. In his book *The Culture Cycle: How to Shape the Unseen Force that Transforms Performance* (Pearson FT Press, 2015), James Heskett claims that a coherent and effective culture can generate as much as a 30% difference in performance as compared to a 'culturally unremarkable' competitor.

According to their website, www.adobe.com, Adobe, the award-winning software company, has four core values – genuine, exceptional, innovative and involved. Each value has a detailed description behind it, as well as programmes investing in the company's people and the communities they live in. Virgin, another award-winning company, describes its values on its website, www.virgin.com, as 'providing heartfelt service, being delightfully surprising, red hot, and straight up while maintaining an insatiable curiosity and creating smart disruption'.

Your values are what will help guide all the decisions you make and the actions you take in your business. It's important that you hire, manage and reward people in line with these values and that you don't retain anyone who's acting against them. In this chapter, we'll look at core human values, communication and conflict.

Core human values

Depending on which piece of research or article you read, the core human values that we all hold dear are expressed a little differently.

Glenn Martin, author of *Human Values and Ethics in the Workplace* (Lulu.com, 2011), says that the core human values are truth, peace, right action, love and insight. Tony Robbins, life coach and author of *Awaken the Giant Within: How to Take Immediate Control of Your Mental, Emotional, Physical and Financial Life* (Simon & Schuster, 2012), expresses them as certainty, variety, significance, love and connection, growth and contribution.

With an eye on applying these values to business, I believe that our core human needs can be expressed as follows:

- To make a difference

- To discover and grow

- To engage and connect

- To be happy

- To be trusted and revered

One of these is your core ideal. You may hold several of these, but one is dominant. You may have two that are very close – if so, which one feels like your core value? For example, if you feel that both 'discover and grow' and 'make a difference' are important to you, I would ask you to consider whether you're making a difference so you can discover and grow or whether you're discovering and growing in order to make a difference.

Many companies are recruiting based on a values fit rather than a cultural fit. John Down of The Dots says, 'We use values as our primary assessor framework. We don't use culture. If you recruit with culture as your primary lodestone, you do end up with a team of people who think like you or just like to go to the pub together. Those things are wonderful but it's not very good for the kind of cognitive diversity that you need when you're operating in a new market like ours.'

Communication

Communication is so important that it could appear in almost any chapter of this book. My experience is that founders almost always underestimate the amount of communication that's required as their businesses grow.

Scott Erwin of Hire Hand told me that he has some sympathy for some of the larger companies in the 'gig economy' that get a bad rap for how they treat their employees. 'They probably started with good intentions,' he told me, 'but then lost their way in terms of managing the complexities of scale and maintaining meaningful engagement with the users of their rapidly growing platform.'

The reason that communication appears in the values part of the REAL model® is that telling people what to do and what's happening will only get you so far. If you tell people *why* you're asking them to do a certain thing, or *why* the management team has made a certain decision, you have the opportunity to gain their commitment and buy-in at a much more fundamental level. Giving people context is vital. You may understand what's happening and why at a senior management level, but don't forget that others in your business don't have the same access to information as you do. If people don't understand, they'll quickly switch off.

As Julian Cork of Landbay says, 'Unless you build the company right from day zero, in terms of cultural governance, then you won't be able to continue to scale. The wheels fall off if you're not able to get everyone to understand what's happening.' His colleague, John Goodall, told me that he feels strongly about getting people to talk to each other rather than emailing! He said that things easily get misinterpreted when communicated via email, and that he's determined to build a culture of good communication in Landbay, using regular stand-up meetings to assess how people are doing and town hall meetings to explain not just the priorities of the company but also the reasons behind these priorities. He told me that he thinks 'the importance of getting buy-in, even from senior positions, is underestimated'. He believes that communicating not just what they're doing but also why is becoming more and more important as they grow. 'Rightly or wrongly, when you're small, the assumption is that people "get it" more.'

John and Pip of The Dots cited communication as a key reason why they didn't want to introduce too much hierarchy into their business. They explained that if their account managers weren't able to influence product development in real time, they wouldn't be able to innovate and deliver a better product to their clients. They credit their ability to maintain flexibility and communication as the company grows to their use of OKRs (see the Metrics chapter).

Clive Rich of LawBite told me that his Monday morning management meeting is the most important meeting of the week. 'I think it's important everyone understands what we're doing, why we're doing it, and is aligned with us at the beginning of the week.'

Recognising and resolving conflict

Even though as entrepreneurs, we have more choice than employees over who we spend time with, we all encounter drama or conflict in our lives from time to time. In the Further Reading section, I've included some links to more detailed information on Karpman's Drama Triangle. This is a useful model to understand how drama plays out between people in conflict – work colleagues, business partners or family members.

The Drama Triangle describes three roles that we can play in a conflict situation – the persecutor, the victim and the rescuer. We'll usually have one that we fall most naturally into, but interestingly, these roles aren't fixed, so we can shift, especially if new people join what Karpman calls the 'game'. We can move endlessly around the triangle during a conflict – first shouting out our opinion, then feeling 'got-at' when we're challenged and then rescuing our former adversaries when they start feeling vulnerable. It's a rotating pattern of co-dependent behaviours that ultimately serves no one. Each player gets their unspoken and often unconscious needs met in a selfish way that they feel is justified without having to acknowledge the damage being done. It continues until someone chooses to exit.

As the triangle starts with people getting too involved in what other people are doing, stepping out means taking responsibility for our own actions, feelings and needs. Karpman tells us that the way to step out of the triangle is to become aware of the game and the role we're playing in it and then simply step out and ask for what we need – calmly and rationally. As the game requires multiple players, be aware that people will get upset when you choose to exit, but as a real entrepreneur, you'll need to learn how to recognise what's going on in your team and your business so that you can take a step back before trying to resolve the situation.

The following is a useful tool to use when looking to resolve a conflict. Make sure you've stepped out of the Drama Triangle before you start.

Conflict resolution tool

1. Talk with the other person – ask for their help to resolve the conflict

2. Focus on events and behaviours rather than personalities

3. Listen carefully

4. Admit mistakes

5. Identify points of commonality and difference

6. Prioritise

7. Develop a plan that you both agree to

8. Follow through

9. Keep talking regularly

Speaking your truth is a key part of staying true to your values. Whenever you fail to do so, you compromise yourself and, in turn, your business. A values fit is usually more important than any other quality when it comes to people working together.

Values – Top three takeaways

1. As your business grows, you'll need to communicate more than you think is necessary

2. Give people context – tell them *why* the company is doing what it's doing

3. Speaking your truth and asking for what you need enables you to stay true to your values and resolve conflicts

CHAPTER TWELVE

Plan

'You don't have to be great to start, but you have to start to be great.'

— Zig Ziglar, American author and speaker

In business, things rarely go according to plan. A new hire doesn't work out, a piece of equipment fails or a client cancels a contract. As businesses grow, many lose their way without even realising it. There's an initial momentum that comes from creating products or services, finding customers, and delivering, but once that has passed, it can easily be replaced with endless rounds of firefighting – reacting to the latest crisis, responding to each new demand. Every day there's a new priority, a new focus for the team, something else which is of critical importance, until it isn't anymore.

There are many reasons why the best laid plans fail – here are some of the most common:

1. Over-optimism or commercial pressure

2. Failure to learn from previous mistakes

3. Illusion of control

4. Narrow focus

5. Complexity

6. Black swans, ie completely unexpected events (see the Further Reading section for a book on this phenomenon)

Many people see planning as the very opposite of creativity, a way to crush dreams, restrict possibilities and kill spontaneity. They object to the perceived restriction of having to decide what they're going to do and then sticking to it. Others find the whole process tedious and pointless. One of the reasons we can find it a challenge is that as soon as we set ourselves a goal, there's a tension created between where we are today and where we want to be. So it may not be the planning that's causing us stress but the desire to reach our goal.

The bottom line is that if you don't do any kind of planning, you'll never make it, unless by coincidence and chance.

Plan – Map the journey

Planning allows you to set direction and priorities, and it gets everyone on the same page. It also helps simplify decision-making and drives alignment. When I talk about planning, I don't mean writing a detailed business plan – I mean laying out a course that you want to follow, knowing who's going to do what and having a guide to measure yourself by. I agree with Carl Schramm, author of *Burn the Business Plan: What Great Entrepreneurs Really Do* (John Murray, 2018), when he argues that the time constraints in most business plans can blind businesses to what's really happening, especially when they have investors breathing down their necks, holding them to dates. None of us know what's going to happen. We can map out the journey and start on our way knowing where we're heading, but trying to predict timelines can be fraught with problems.

Clive Rich of LawBite told me that there's a constant challenge around priorities. 'How much time do you dedicate to the future, and how much to the here and now, when it seems like the here and now is all that matters? But actually, we know that it isn't.' In this chapter, we'll look at how to plan, how to avoid planning mistakes and some alternatives to the traditional business plan.

How to plan

As adults, we like to make things complicated. In the interests of keeping things simple, here's how I advise teams to plan.

Planning tool

Use flip-chart paper and different-coloured sticky notes.

1. **Determine objectives** – Agree on the objectives for the business (or team) for the period ahead (month, quarter, year). Write each one on a sticky note (make sure all the sticky notes are the same colour). Be really clear about where you're going and what you're trying to achieve. *'What are the exact outcomes we're looking for and are they measurable? How will we know when we achieve our goal? Where are we today? Where are we starting from?'*

2. **Determine constraints** – Discuss what obstacles you face as a team in meeting your objectives. Capture them on sticky notes (use a different colour this time) and align them with the objectives that they may block. Get clear about exactly what's standing in the way of progress. *'What are our limitations in terms of time, money, resources, etc.? What could stop us achieving our goals?'*

3. **Determine actions** – Write a list of all the actions you'll need to take to achieve the objectives and overcome the obstacles. Capture these on sticky notes (a third colour) and group them with the objectives and constraints. Get as many options as possible written down without any judgement or discussion. *'What options do we have? What actions could we take?'*

4. **Prioritise** – Review the list of actions – challenge, prioritise and refine. Focus on the ones that are essential to achieving your objectives or overcoming obstacles. *'Which options overlap? Which ones do we choose? Which are our backup actions?'*

5. **Organise** – Put the actions into a list according to the order they'll get done. Work out which ones are dependent on others being completed first. Discuss the most logical or efficient way to get each of them done. *'How do we organise our chosen actions? What order should they be done in?'*

6. **Resource** – Assign names to each action. Adjust your plan as you take into account workload and capacity, but still keep focus on which actions need to take priority to move you towards your objective. *'Who should perform each task?'*

7. **Adjust** – A plan is a living, breathing document. It should be referred to often, updated regularly and challenged by everyone involved. The team should ask themselves regularly what new information they have and how it might impact

the plan. *'How often shall we review our plan? What are our methods of adapting it and keeping it up-to-date and relevant?'*

In the Resilience section of this book, we looked at how to learn from mistakes. Here's how to avoid the most common planning mistakes.

Avoiding planning mistakes

1. To avoid over-optimism or commercial pressure, get a colleague or different team to review the plan and provide formal feedback.

2. Always conduct a 'lessons learned' session at the end of every project and review them as part of putting together the plan.

3. We often believe that we can control things that we can't, so it's important to look at the plan and try to identify its points of potential failure.

4. To combat a focus that's too narrow, ensure that proper research has been conducted into markets, competition, etc. – whatever is relevant to inform the plan.

5. We often underestimate the resources, time or budget that we'll need to cope with dependencies, such as teams working together, relying on outside suppliers or negotiating a contract. The only solution here is to try to simplify the plan as much as possible to avoid unnecessary complexity and interdependencies.

6. Black swans by their very nature are unexpected and impossible to plan for. When we plan, we tend to ignore the possibility of something happening that we can't see today. It's vital that the objectives of the plan are clear – 'What is it that we're trying to achieve here?' As long as this is clear, an adjusted or new plan can be created.

The key with planning is to be flexible. Use your plan as a guide rather than a pair of handcuffs or a mill-stone around your neck.

Alternatives to the traditional business plan

The traditional business plan is a book that's out of date the minute you finish it. Trying to run your fast-moving business by a book that you wrote before you started is usually a waste of your time. The critical thing is to know where you're going so you can keep the team together and focused and so you can track progress.

If you put the following elements together, a formal business plan is unlikely to be needed.

Instead of a business plan

1. **Success document.** One or two pages that describes what success looks like – where you're going and the numbers you want to hit. Think of it as a strategy summary rather than a business plan.

2. **Project management tool.** Find the one that works for you – Trello, Basecamp, Asana. It keeps people accountable and promotes transparency and collaboration.

3. **Calendar.** Use your calendar to plan out your time and ensure you meet deadlines.

4. **Note taker.** Whether you use a notes tool like OneNote or a spreadsheet, make sure you keep yourself accountable by tracking your ideas, random thoughts, goals and progress.

Even the best laid plans go awry. As a real entrepreneur, you'll need to keep calm, ask for help, involve your team, make corrections and, when necessary, come up with a new plan.

Plan – Top three takeaways

1. Having a plan means that you know where you're going and can track your progress along the way

2. Knowing your objective is critical to keep you focused on the end game

3. Use planning as a means to an end rather than an end in itself

---

Bringing Leadership together

Leadership is about knowing what you're building and why. A clear vision leads to congruency and motivation. What will it look and feel like? Why should people care? Why do you care? It's about every member of the team aligning themselves with the heart and soul of the business. Scott Erwin of Hire Hand told me he's a firm believer that 'leadership is not based on hierarchy'. Leadership is needed at all levels of your organisation – people stepping up and doing great things for your business model, customers or culture. Staying true to who you are and encouraging the people around you to do the same will be the keys to your business's success. Using your values as a guide through challenging decisions will help you stay on track, so you don't wake up one day and not recognise or value what you've built. Being a real entrepreneur is about the desire to fix a problem – it's about having a clear picture of what the solution looks like, charting a course to a destination and pulling in good people around you to help you achieve your vision. The best thing you can do for your people as their leader is to ask them 'What is the one thing I could do that would help you be more in flow, enable you to be more productive and make you want to stay in this business?' and then really listen. Nothing puts people in flow quite like someone who's really paying attention and really hearing them.

- What are your key takeaways from the Leadership section?

- What are you going to implement immediately?

- What are you looking at differently now?

Conclusion

'You can do anything, if you stop trying to do everything.'

— Oliver Emberton, British founder of Silktide

Running a business is one of the most exhilarating, frustrating and life-changing experiences that anyone can have. For Sally, the lady who loved to sew, it was a journey from trying to do everything herself, to feeling overwhelmed, to asking for help, realising that the answer lay in *who* not *how* and then back to focusing on what put her in flow. This is different for each and every one of us, but finding what it is and then sticking to it is the key to business and personal success.

Think of an aeroplane and how it travels. The space near the jet stream is where you're likely to find the most turbulence. Similarly, when you feel out of sorts or frustrated, it's important to ask yourself if you're getting close to your flow or if you're simply doing the wrong thing – the two can feel similar at times.

Throughout this book, as I've taken you through my REAL model®, I've emphasised what I believe to be the fundamental truths of any business – however long it's been trading and whatever the size, location or industry:

- Business is a team sport – you don't need to know it all and you don't have to do it all

- Be where you are in the journey – it's not a race

- Play to your strengths and speak your truth

- Asking for help is the most important thing you can do

I hope that this book has given you some useful tools to deal with the journey ahead, whether you're at the start or several years in. But more than that, I hope that you now know what it means to be a real entrepreneur – a resilient, energised, accountable leader.

If you get stuck, head over to my website and book a call with me. We'll look at one area you're unclear on, one tool that you want to explore further or one issue that you need some perspective on.

I hope that, like Sally, you rediscover what made you want to be an entrepreneur and fall in love with your business all over again. Above all I hope that you build a business that works for you.

Further Reading

Resilience resources
Resilience links

'Burned Out? This 1 Habit Will Ensure You Never Burn Out Again' by Nicolas Cole (The Ascent, 19 Aug 2018) https://theascent.pub/burned-out-this-1-habit-will-ensure-you-never-burn-out-again-b73d2e6fff8b

'Talking About Failure Is Crucial For Growth. Here's How to Do It Right' by Oset Babur (*New York Times*, 17 August 2018) www.nytimes.com/2018/08/17/smarter-living/talking-about-failure-is-crucial-for-growth-heres-how-to-do-it-right.html

'Why is entrepreneurship such an emotional rollercoaster?' by Daniel Priestley, (LinkedIn, 18 July 2017) www. linkedin.com/pulse/why-entrepreneurship-emotional-roller-coaster-daniel-priestley/

'Elon Musk Details "Excruciating" Personal Toll of Tesla Turmoil' by David Gelles, James B. Stewart, Jessica Silver-Greenberg, Kate Kelly (*New York Times*, 16 Aug 2018) www.nytimes.com/2018/08/16/business/elon-musk-interview-tesla.html

'Elon Musk's Week from Hell Ends with Tears' by Maya Kosoff (*Vanity Fair*, 17 August 2018) www. vanityfair.com/news/2018/08/elon-musks-week-from-hell-ends-with-tears

'An Open Letter to Elon Musk' by Arianna Huffington (Thrive Global, 17 Aug 2018) www.thriveglobal. com/stories/40343-open-letter-elon-musk

'The Morning Routine of 15 Successful Entrepreneurs' by Belle Cooper (Foundr, 13 March 2017) https://foundr. com/morning-routine-entrepreneurs/

'Eric Berne Memorial Scientific Award Lecture' by Stephen Karpman (Karpman Drama Triangle, 1972) www.karpmandramatriangle.com/pdf/Award Speech.pdf

'Blame Culture vs. Fail Culture; What's your company's?' by Jean-Pierre Lambert (JP Lambert, 7 May 2018)

https://jp-lambert.me/blame-culture-vs-fail-culture-whats-your-company-s-52568738e686

'*Managing the Costs of Clinical Negligence in Trusts*' by the Comptroller and Auditor General (National Audit Office, 7 September 2017) www.nao.org.uk/wp-content/uploads/2017/09/Managing-the-costs-of-clinical-negligence-in-trusts.pdf

'*Being Vulnerable about Vulnerability*' by Brene Brown (*TED Blog*, 16 March 2012) https://blog.ted.com/being-vulnerable-about-vulnerability-qa-with-brene-brown/

'*Do You Suffer From Decision Fatigue?*' by John Tierney (*New York Times*, 17 Aug 2011) www.nytimes.com/2011/08/21/magazine/do-you-suffer-from-decision-fatigue.html

'*The scientific reason why Barack Obama and Mark Zuckerberg wear the same outfit every day*' by Drake Baer (Business Insider, 28 April 2015) http://uk.businessinsider.com/barack-obama-mark-zuckerberg-wear-the-same-outfit-2015-4?r=US&IR=T

'*Extraneous factors in judicial decisions*' by Shai Danziger, Jonathan Levav and Liora Avnaim-Pesso, (PNAS, 25 February 2011) www.pnas.org/content/pnas/108/17/6889.full.pdf

'The psychology of doing nothing: Forms of decision avoidance result from reason and emotion' by Christopher Anderson (Psycnet, Jan 2003) http://psycnet.apa.org/doiLanding?doi=10.1037%2F0033-2909.129.1.139

'Taking the scenic route' by Carl Martin (Medium, 19 April 2018) https://medium.com/@carlmartin/taking-the-scenic-route-c7ba89e8aae2

'How To Creatively Celebrate Your Team's Wins' by Chris Myers, (Forbes, 16 December 2016) www.forbes.com/sites/chrismyers/2016/12/16/how-to-creatively-celebrate-your-teams-wins/#2be9b370290e

Resilience books

The Miracle Morning: The 6 Habits That Will Transform Your Life Before 8AM' by Hal Elrod (John Murray, 2016).

Remove the Guesswork: The Highly Personalised Approach to Health, Fitness and Nutrition That Puts You First' by Leanne Spencer (Rethink Press, 2016).

'The Lean Startup: How Constant Innovation Creates Radically Successful Businesses' by Eric Ries (Penguin, 2011)

'Willpower Doesn't Work: Discover the Hidden Keys to Success' by Benjamin Hardy (Piatkus, 2018)

'*The Fifth Discipline: The Art and Practice of the Learning Organization*' by Peter Senge (Cornerstone Digital, 2010)

'*Black Box Thinking: The Surprising Truth About Success*' by Matthew Syed (John Murray, 2015)

'*Your Best Year Yet: Make the Next 12 months Your Best Ever!*' by Jinny Ditzler (HarperElement, 2012)

'*The Progress Principle: Using Small Wins to Ignite Joy, Engagement and Creativity at Work*' by Teresa Amabile and Steven Kramer (Harvard Business Review Press, 2011)

'*How to be Happy: How Developing Your Confidence, Resilience, Appreciation and Communication Can Lead to a Happier, Healthier You*' by Liggy Webb (John Wiley & Sons, 2012)

'*Better Than Before: Mastering the Habits of Our Everyday Lives*' by Gretchen Rubin (Two Roads, 2015)

'*Find your Flexible Warrior: Think, Stretch and Eat for Balance and Resilience*' by Karen Dubs (Flexible Warrior Publications, 2015)

'*The 5 Second Rule: Transform Your Life, Work and Confidence with Everyday Courage*' by Mel Robbins (Savio Republic, 2017)

'*Why We Sleep: The New Science of Sleep and Dreams*' by Matthew Walker (Penguin, 2017)

'*Sleep Smarter: 21 Essential Strategies to Sleep Your Way to a Better Body, Better Health and Bigger Success*' by Shawn Stevenson (Hay House UK, 2016)

'*The Chimp Paradox: The Acclaimed Mind Management Programme to Help You Achieve Success, Confidence and Happiness*' by Steve Peters (Ebury Digital, 2012)

'*The Power of Habit: Why We Do What We Do, and How to Change*' by Charles Duhigg (Cornerstone Digital, 2012)

'*Slow Burn: Burn Fat Faster By Exercising Slower*' by Stu Mittleman and Katherine Callan (William Morrow Paperbacks, 2011)

'*The Nature Fix: Why Nature Makes Us Happier, Healthier and More Creative*' by Florence Williams (W. W. Norton & Company, 2018)

Energy resources

Energy links

'*How to Maintain a State of Creative 'Flow'*' by Corey McComb (Medium, 20 Aug 2018) https://medium.com/s/story/how-to-master-the-flow-state-one-simple-yet-difficult-trick-56854fca9109

'Uber CEO says company is "actively looking for" a new chief operating officer' by Anita Balakrishnan (CNBC, 7 March 2017) www.cnbc.com/2017/03/07/uber-looking-for-chief-operating-officer.html 'Psychometrics' (GeniusU)

www.geniusu.com/psychometrics

'River of Wealth' by Roger Hamilton (GeniusU, 30 June 2013) www.geniusu.com/articles/3871588

'Why Niching Down is the Most Important Business Decision You'll Make' by Megan Brame (Huffington Post, 8 December 2017) www.huffingtonpost.com/megan-bramefinkelstein/why-niching-down-is-the-m_b_13488246.html

'3 Lies You Need to Stop Believing About Finding a Niche' by Kat Boogaard (INC, 20 October 2017 www.inc.com/kat-boogaard/3-myths-about-niching-down-your-business-debunked.html

'The riches are in the niches' by Neville Chamberlain (Multiplier, 13 December 2017) https://medium.com/multiplier-magazine/the-riches-are-in-the-niches-98db3872706f

'How boredom can lead to your most brilliant ideas' by Manoush Zomorodi (TED, April 2017) www.ted.com/talks/manoush_zomorodi_how_boredom_can_lead_to_your_most_brilliant_ideas

Energy books

'*The 7 Habits of Highly Effective People: Powerful Lessons in Personal Change*' by Stephen Covey (Rosetta Books, 2013)

'*Abundance: The Future Is Better Than You Think*' by Peter Diamandis and Steven Kotler (Free Press, 2012)

'*The Culture Code: The Secrets of Highly Successful Groups*' by Daniel Coyle (Cornerstone Digital, 2018)

'*Quiet: The Power of Introverts in a World That Can't Stop Talking*' by Susan Cain (Penguin, 2012)

'*Niche Down: How to Become Legendary By Being Different*' by Christopher Lochhead and Heather Clancy (Christopher Lochhead & Heather Clancy, 2018)

'*The 80/20 Principle: The Secret of Achieving More with Less*' by Richard Koch (Nicholas Brealey Publishing, 1998)

'*How to Win Friends and Influence People*' by Dale Carnegie (Ebury Digital, 2010)

'*Stealing Fire: How Silicon Valley, the Navy SEALs and Maverick Scientists Are Revolutionizing the Way We Live and Work*' by Steven Kotler and Jamie Wheal (Dey Street Books, 2017)

'On Form: Managing Energy, Not Time, is the Key to High Performance, Health and Happiness' by Jim Loehr and Tony Schwartz (Nicholas Brealey Publishing, 2011)

'The Effortless Experience: Conquering the New Battleground for Customer Loyalty' by Matthew Dixon, Nick Toman and Rick DeLisi (Penguin, 2013)

'Leading at a Higher Level: Blanchard on How to be a High Performing Leader' by Ken Blanchard (Financial Times/Prentice Hall, 2010)

'Expert Secrets: The Underground Playbook for Creating a Mass Movement of People Who Will Pay for Your Advice' by Russell Brunson (Morgan James Publishing, 2017)

Accountability resources

Accountability links

'7 Types of Organizational Structure & Whom They're Suited For' by Erik Devaney (Hubspot Blog, 10 December 2018) https://blog.hubspot.com/marketing/team-structure-diagrams

'When your boss is an algorithm' by Sarah O'Connor (Financial Times, 8 September 2016) www.ft.com/content/88fdc58e-754f-11e6-b60a-de4532d5ea35?segmentid=acee4131-99c2-09d3-a635-873e61754ec6

'How to Manage People Who Know More Than You' by Katie Douthwaite Wolf (The Muse) www.themuse. com/advice/how-to-manage-people-who-know-more-than-you

Accountability books

'*Oversubscribed: How to Get People Lining Up to Do Business with You*' by Daniel Priestley (Capstone, 2015)

'*The E-Myth Revisited*' by Michael Gerber (HarperCollins, 2009)

'*Scaling Up: How a Few Companies Make It... and Why the Rest Don't*' by Verne Harnish (Gazelles, 2014)

'*Process to Profit – systemise your business to build a high performing team and gain more time, more control and more profit*' by Marianne Page (Rethink Press, 2013)

'*Traction: Get a Grip on Your Business*' by Gino Wickman (BenBella, 2012)

'*Managing Oneself*' by Peter Drucker (Harvard Business Review Press, 2008)

'*Measure What Matters: OKRs – The Simple Idea that Drives 10x Growth*' by John Doerr (Penguin, 2018)

'*The Big Short: Inside the Doomsday Machine*' by Michael Lewis (Penguin, 2011)

'Built to Sell: Creating a Business That Can Thrive Without You' by John Warrillow and Bo Burlingham (Portfolio, 2011)

'Maverick: The Success Story Behind the World's Most Unusual Workplace' by Ricardo Semler (Random House Business, 2001)

'It Doesn't Have to be Crazy at Work' by Jason Fried and David Hansson (HarperCollins, 2018)

Leadership resources

Leadership links

'Know Your Why' by Michael Jr. (YouTube, 8 January 2017) www.youtube.com/watch?v=1ytFB8TrkTo

'How Corporate Culture Affects the Bottom Line' by Jillian Popadak, John Graham, Campbell Harvey and Shiva Rajgopal (Fuqua Duke, 12 November 2015) www.fuqua.duke.edu/duke-fuqua-insights/corporate-culture#.V7F-R5N97os

'Why People Really Quit Their Jobs' by Lori Goler, Janella Gale, Brynn Harrington and Adam Grant (*Harvard Business Review*, 11 January 2018) https://hbr.org/2018/01/why-people-really-quit-their-jobs

'*Tony Robbins: 6 Basic Needs That Make Us Tick*' by Tony Robbins (Entrepreneur, 4 December 2014) www.entrepreneur.com/article/240441

'*Core human values and the Chinese elements*' by Glenn Martin (*Ethics and Values*, 2005) www.ethicsandvalues.com.au/files/chvelements.pdf

'*The* 'No Plan' *Business Plan for Entrepreneurs*' by Kevin Kruse (Forbes, 30 July 2018) www.forbes.com/sites/kevinkruse/2018/07/30/the-no-plan-business-plan-for-entrepreneurs/#74c0bd6c55e5

'*How to start a movement*' by Derek Sivers (TED, February 2010) www.ted.com/talks/derek_sivers_how_to_start_a_movement/up-next

'*How to Achieve Your Most Ambitious Goals*' by Stephen Duneier (YouTube, 6 March 2017) www.youtube.com/watch?v=TQMbvJNRpLE

Leadership books

'*Start with Why: How Great Leaders Inspire Everyone to Take Action*' by Simon Sinek (Penguin, 2011)

'*Good to Great*' by Jim Collins (Random House Business, 2001)

'*Entrepreneur Revolution: How to Develop your Entrepreneurial Mindset and Start a Business that Works*' by Daniel Priestley (Capstone, 2018)

'*Play Bigger: How Rebels and Innovators Create New Categories and Dominate Markets*' by Al Ramandan, Dave Peterson, Christopher Lochhead and Kevin Maney (Piatkus, 2016)

'*The Art of War*' by Sun Tzu (LBA, 2019)

'*The Culture Cycle: How to Shape the Unseen Force that Transforms Performance*' by James Heskett (Pearson FT Press, 2015)

'*Awaken the Giant Within: How to Take Immediate Control of Your Mental, Emotional, Physical and Financial Life*' by Tony Robbins (Simon & Schuster, 2012)

'*Burn the Business Plan: What Great Entrepreneurs Really Do*' by Carl Schramm (John Murray, 2018)

'*Factfulness: Ten Reasons We're Wrong About The World – And Why Things Are Better Than You Think*' by Hans Rosling (Sceptre, 2018)

'*Sapiens: A Brief History of Humankind*' by Yuval Noah Harari (Vintage Digital, 2014)

'*The Surrender Experiment: My Journey into Life's Perfection*' by Michael Singer (Yellow Kite, 2015)

'*Second to None: How Our Smartest Companies Put People First*' by Charles Garfield (Illinois, 1992)

Acknowledgements

I have been incredibly fortunate throughout my life to have encountered people who recognised something in me that I couldn't yet see myself. John Sollesse helped me avoid a life of selling yoghurt and steered me in the direction of Xerox, the most wonderful environment to learn and develop my skills. Gennady German spotted the implementer in me at a time where I was sure that I would soon get 'found out' for not being strategic enough. Thomas Herrmann knew I could help him transform the reputation of a leading investment bank, and brought me in to manage teams and projects, when many questioned the value of someone with absolutely no credit risk knowledge. And Paul Avins continues to patiently and generously show me what is possible in this wonderful world of the entrepreneur – reminding me, when I doubt myself, that having an outside perspective is a valuable quality to bring to my clients.

Many people have helped with the creation of this book but special mention must go to those people who gave generously of their time to be interviewed: Juliet and Carl from Any Good?, Pip and John from The Dots, Clive and Richard from LawBite, Paul and Julia from Whyte & Co, John and Julian from Landbay, and Scott from Hire Hand. I also had the benefit of amazing beta readers who gave me really insightful and challenging feedback on my draft manuscripts. It would not be the book it is without their inputs. My heartfelt thanks go to Martin, Rachel, Jerry, Graham, Francesca, Jan, Corinne, Andy, Sian and Isobel. No book gets published without a team of people bringing it all together. Lucy and Joe and their great team at Rethink Press make the whole process feel easy and were a joy to work with.

I doubt I would have written a book if it wasn't for my great friend and business partner, Andy, dragging me along to something called a Brand Accelerator day, run by Dent Global. Friday 31 March 2017 opened my eyes and changed my life. It was the start of an incredible rollercoaster ride during which I've met so many wonderful and inspiring individuals and learned more about myself then I ever thought possible. Andy continues to provide me with great perspective and shades of grey whenever I get stuck in a 'black and white' mindset.

And finally, I want to pay tribute to my wonderful mother, Cilla, who taught me that anything and everything is possible, who gently corrected me if I ever used the word 'should' and who gave me the confidence to go out into the world and live life on my terms. When I set off to university, never once did she show a flicker of how hard it was for her to let her eldest go and when I trained as a Lean Six Sigma Black Belt, she proudly told her neighbours that her daughter was a 'business ninja' without having a clue what that meant. When I left the UK riding a motorcycle that would carry me 12,000 miles through Eastern Europe all the way to India and on into the jungles of Cambodia and Laos, she offered a very mild enquiry about how safe it was to ride through Pakistan and Iran in September 2001! She kept her calm when I called from the hospital in Thailand to tell her that I had broken my ankle and was being operated on, and whenever I announce that my husband and I are planning another scuba diving trip to some tiny island in the middle of nowhere, she takes it in her stride. She is a remarkable woman who encourages me to be me. No strings, no expectations, no judgement.

I consider myself lucky to have loved every single job I've done in my life and I believe passionately that everyone deserves to love what they do. Throughout my life, whenever I've met anyone who is doing something that doesn't light them up inside, it has hurt me deeply and I always feel compelled to challenge as well as to try and help them find their way. When my wonderful friend Isobel persuaded me to attend an event about life coaching, I was determined not to get sucked into their sales patter! I sat in that room in August 2017 and knew that I'd come home. After so many years of searching, I had found my purpose. My greatest wish for you is that you find yours.

The Author

 Lisa Zevi started her career at Xerox where she learned many of the managerial, sales, operational and project management skills that she uses today. Her experience as a 'right-hand woman' working in large corporates and investment banks meant that she saw first-hand the power of collaborative partnerships between impatient, ambitious visionaries and people who were born to implement. She uses her experience to help entrepreneurs form great partnerships that drive businesses forward.

She is a qualified business coach, Team Dynamics Partner and Lean Six Sigma Black Belt, and is passionate about encouraging business owners to play to their strengths, grow great teams and build businesses that work for them.

Learn more at www.lisazevi.com